BRIDGE BUILDING APOLOGETICS

LINDSEY MEDENWALDT

HARVEST HOUSE PUBLISHERS
EUGENE, OREGON

Cover design by Faceout Studio, Elisha Zepeda

Cover illustration hand-drawn by Elisha Zepeda / Faceout Studio

Interior design by KUHN Design Group

For bulk, special sales, or ministry purchases, please call 1-800-547-8979.
Email: CustomerService@hhpbooks.com

Bridge-Building Apologetics
Copyright © 2024 by Lindsey Medenwaldt
Published by Harvest House Publishers
Eugene, Oregon 97408
www.harvesthousepublishers.com

ISBN 978-0-7369-8832-2 (pbk)
ISBN 978-0-7369-8833-9 (eBook)

Library of Congress Control Number: 2023947038

Printed in the United States of America

24 25 26 27 28 29 30 31 32 / BP / 10 9 8 7 6 5 4 3 2 1

"The apostle Paul became 'all things to all people...for the sake of the gospel' (1 Corinthians 9:22-23). And Peter told us to 'always be prepared to give an answer to everyone' who asks about the reason for our hope in Christ (1 Peter 3:15). In this encouraging book, Lindsey Medenwaldt presents a wealth of practical ideas to help us do both—relate to people as friends and present to them the truth of our faith. Read it for ideas and inspiration, and don't miss chapter 9 on building friendships. It's worth the price of the entire book!"

—**Mark Mittelberg**, author of *Contagious Faith* and *Confident Faith*; executive director of the Strobel Center, Colorado Christian University

"After decades of experience in apologetics, I often lament that so many unbelievers are ignorant of apologetics because Christians often lack the intellectual and relational skills needed to bring the case for Christianity to unbelievers. This book is a welcome and much-needed antidote to that problem. Through its use of Scripture, personal experiences, culture, and apologetic savvy, *Bridge-Building Apologetics* equips Christians to 'contend for the faith that was once for all delivered to the saints' (Jude 3 ESV)."

—**Douglas Groothuis**, Professor of Philosophy, Denver Seminary; author of *Christian Apologetics: A Comprehensive Case for Biblical Faith*

"Evangelism and apologetics can become harsh and alienating in the hands of some people. In contrast, Lindsey Medenwaldt's book shows us how to relate to non-Christians in a biblical and loving manner. She emphasizes that evangelism is a spiritual struggle, and that as Christians we need to build a strong foundation in our relationships with God and others so that the Holy Spirit will open people's hearts to the gospel. Her writing style is engaging, and her catchy references to contemporary culture make it difficult to put the book down."

—**Winfried Corduan**, Professor Emeritus of Philosophy and Religion, Taylor University

"Lindsey delivers a timely message full of creative examples to help us see every person as God's image bearers who deserve to hear the truth with gentleness and respect. Connecting the head and the heart, *Bridge Building Apologetics* will encourage you to evaluate your approach to evangelism and apologetics with humility."

—**Rachel Shockey,** president of Women in Apologetics

"Too often, we characterize apologetics as a weapon deployed for combat. Representatives of alternative views engage one another as pugilists instead of image-bearers worthy of respect. Attempts to defend our faith can devolve into intellectual one-upmanship at the expense of fervor for lost souls. Such an approach undermines apologetics by neglecting its intent.

"In *Bridge-Building Apologetics*, Lindsey Medenwaldt, my dear friend, presents an apologetic for relational apologetics. Shamelessly, she values advocating for the historic Christian faith, but never at the expense of human dignity. For her, apologetics is an essential tool of evangelism. This book is a convicting work that should bear on our apologetic methods. I commend it to every believer who desires to be a witness and defender of our faith."

—**Brandon Washington,** lead pastor, Embassy Christian Bible Church

To Jay

ACKNOWLEDGMENTS

To God. You get all the glory. All. Of. It.

To Jay. For believing in me and for encouraging me to keep pushing. What a gift it has been to know you. I'll be forever grateful for your support and love.

To my daughters. For always understanding when I needed to spend some time writing. I'm honored and blessed to be your mom. Now, let's go get some ice cream and cupcakes.

To my parents. For encouraging me to persist and for reminding me of God's great blessings in my life.

To my editor, Steve, and his wife, Becky. For your care. What a joy it has been to work with you. Thank you for taking a chance on me and for bearing with me.

To my fellow Mama Bears and our prayer team. For inspiring me to keep writing, even when the days were long and the words were few.

To Teri. For hooking me up with a place to retreat and write. That week saved this book. One heart, one way.

To Bethany and McKenzie. For the gift package you sent with me on my first writing retreat.

To Adam. For letting me borrow some of your books for months on end. That's true friendship.

To Heather, Jamie, and Denise. Your friendship and support during this crazy process was more essential in my life than you could imagine.

To my Pelican Project sisters. Your advice and support over the last year went above and beyond anything I ever expected. I will always be in your debt.

To Kate. Pomodoro. (That's cheers! for writers.)

To Biscoff. For cookie butter. Writing was much sweeter with a jar of your crunchy cookie butter and a spoon at my desk.

CONTENTS

HILLARY MORGAN FERRER

Lindsey has been a bridge builder since long before *Bridge-Building Apologetics* ever existed. There are plenty of people who write Christian books telling us how we ought to behave as Christians. But take it from me—someone who has worked with her for years—Lindsey embodies everything she talks about in this book.

People of all stripes, colors, and creeds are drawn to Lindsey because of the way she thoughtfully engages with them. Having had her on the Mama Bear Apologetics team for many years, I continue to be impressed with the way she prioritizes listening, curiosity, and kindness with everyone she encounters—and she does it without tiptoeing around key truths that Christianity teaches.

So while this may seem like "just a book" at first glance, it is more than that. It is a discipleship manual written by someone who follows her own advice. The ideas presented are not new, per se. Rather, they are timeless reminders of how we are to conduct ourselves with the people around us. If all Christians would put these very scriptural, very Jesus-like, very simple to understand and commonsense habits into practice, I don't think we as Christians would be the punchline of nearly as many jokes or the focus of so much criticism about our faith. Indeed, there are even atheists who exempt Lindsey from their snarky comments about evangelical Christians (and especially Christian apologists) because of the way she chooses to engage.

In *Bridge-Building Apologetics*, Lindsey reminds us that we don't have to compromise our biblical positions to move forward in relationships. Anyone can maintain a shallow friendship by hiding their faith or refusing to speak biblical truth. Yet we are called to have convictions! We're not called to be wimps for Jesus. So how do we maintain our zeal for Christ and the Bible while still having genuine relationships with those who think differently? Keep reading. It really isn't rocket science, and Lindsey is a good and patient teacher.

God calls all of us to be bridge builders to a world that is separated from Him—while remaining untainted by the world itself. In a day when everyone says and does what is right in their own eyes, Scripture exhorts us to be holy (set apart) by the way we relate to people with whom we disagree. The polarization in our society is getting out of control and we need bridge builders, people filled with living water who are willing to douse the flames of discord. Put this book into practice, friends. Come forth and be set apart!

FINDING THE RIGHT BALANCE WHEN YOU SHARE YOUR FAITH

Friendship is a deep oneness that develops when two people, speaking the truth in love to one another, journey together to the same horizon.

TIM KELLER

im Keller died today.[1] As I write this, I'm wrestling with grief—realizing that we've lost a stalwart of the Christian faith. I've been scrolling through social media, reading tributes from across the globe about Keller's impact:

- "Aside from his teachings and writings, the enduring impact of Tim Keller, for me, will be how graciously and kindly he responded to trolls and people with ill intent on this platform."[2]

- "Thank [you] for finishing well TK There was no reason to be so generous w/ your time, resources, nor w/ your kindness & gentleness during a moment where both seem to be rare. (outside the gospel) Thanks for loving Jesus."[3]

- "Two things I learned from Tim Keller: 1) the power of gentle speech; 2) not to fear hard questions."[4]

- "I am grateful to God for this man and will forever be so. He opened parts of the gospel that I had never seen before. I look forward to meeting Jesus in person more than anything. But I will also thank Him sincerely for sending Tim Keller."[5]

- "Even though apologetics isn't my strong point and I have difficulty following deep theological discussion, Tim Keller (who will be greatly missed) made me interested in these topics because of his inviting posture."[6]

According to these reflections and others that I've read today about Tim Keller, the reason people held him in such high regard is because of how he shared his faith—not rudely or with an "I'm-gonna-getcha" attitude, but with humility, gentleness, and grace. Finding a balance between speaking truth and showing love seemed to be his goal, and he said as much in his book *The Meaning of Marriage*:

> Love without truth is sentimentality; it supports and affirms us but keeps us in denial about our flaws. Truth without love is harshness; it gives us information but in such a way that we cannot really hear it. God's saving love in Christ, however, is marked by both radical truthfulness about who we are and yet also radical, unconditional commitment to us.[7]

Keller's legacy of commitment to both truth and love reached believers and unbelievers, churched and unchurched. Not everyone always agreed with everything he said, and yet, their reflection was positive. For example, Reverend Patrick Mahoney wrote, "Sad to hear of the passing of Tim Keller. A [C]hristian leader whom I greatly admired even when I disagreed with him. His founding of the Gospel Coalition was a powerful tool to bring orthodox evangelical churches back to America's cities."[8] Keller seemed to understand that his mission was to make disciples, and he did so with a passion and love that was recognized by many, even some who disagreed with him.

Unfortunately, Keller's example isn't the mainstream, which is perhaps why his death caused such an outpouring of condolences on social media. We felt this loss because we lost someone important not because of who he was, but what he did for whom he loved, his Savior. I honestly hesitated to write about Keller in this book because I don't want to put anyone on a pedestal. I didn't know Keller personally, nor do I know everything he ever said or wrote or did. What I do know is that based on interviews, books, and podcasts he was a part of, he loved God, he loved people, and he aimed to make disciples. This book is born out of a desire to raise up more Christians who talk the talk and walk the walk.

Talking about my faith hasn't always been easy, but growing up, I'm sure it was easier for me than it probably was for most. I remember getting in trouble in kindergarten because I told a kid he was going to hell if he didn't give his life to Jesus (whoa, I know, but I was a new Christian who was very much on fire and didn't have couth). I also remember reading my Bible with a friend on the school bus and sharing my faith with my friends in high school.

Because I grew up in the church, I thought I had my faith covered. I knew God is real. I knew Jesus died for me. I knew that Jesus told His followers to make disciples. Sharing my worldview with others was supposed to be par for the course. I was a missionary kid and pastor's kid—that had to count for something, right? Wrong. Well, not entirely wrong, just misguided thinking.

Growing up in the church certainly helped, and doing evangelism next to my parents was the kind of experience some people only dream of. I'm grateful for that, but I'm here to tell you it wasn't enough. As

I grew older, I found myself not sharing my faith with others as often as I once did. Not because I was ashamed or afraid of backlash, but because my faith never came up. I was rarely asked to share my hope. People noticed I read my Bible, sure, but they didn't often ask me questions, and I was not offering any answers without being asked.

Then I entered seminary.[9] I went to school to grow closer with my husband, Jay—I was looking for more substantial things to talk about over dinner and knew he enjoyed apologetics.[10] He became a Christian in part because of apologetics. Jay would talk about apologetics, and typically, I would listen with interest but would walk away not fully understanding. I had rationalized that apologetics was good for him but not necessary for me. And I was okay with that until my first apologetics class with Douglas Groothuis, author of the 1,000-page tome *Christian Apologetics*.

At one point during that first class, Dr. Groothuis asked us to interview an unbeliever. We didn't have to answer any questions; we just had to listen and learn. I will be forever grateful to my friend—I'll call her Priscilla—for agreeing to the conversation. It was because of that assignment that I realized I couldn't answer basic questions about my faith, including the most basic question of all: Why do I believe Christianity is true? It was also because of that conversation that the idea for this book was born. Not right away, but over time, I started to understand the importance of building bridges.

During my time at seminary, I read some books about how to engage with others, but I could never quite find what I was looking for in those texts. All too often I read the words *war*, *opponent*, and *battle* mixed in with tips about having discussions about faith. All too rarely have I stumbled upon the words *gentleness*, *relationship*, and *love*.

If you're reading this book, that probably means you're hoping for tips about having real relationships with people. I recently heard the term *missional friendship*—a friendship you enter with the primary goal of sharing your faith. The person becomes your mission. I'm not saying these kinds of relationships are bad, but that's not solely what I talk about in this book. Instead, I'm encouraging you to seek real, authentic relationships with people. The kind that can greatly benefit your life and theirs. Maybe one day you'll get asked about your faith. But maybe you won't. If you do, then this book is going to give you what you need to be ready for that day. The point is, without a real relationship, one with genuine trust and love, you're probably never going to earn a place at the table.

Let me give you an example. Think about Thanksgiving and Christmas. Typically, those holidays are filled with family visits, and so often I hear people say, "Religion and politics always come up at these gatherings." Yep, and you know why? Because of the already-existing relationships in those settings. Usually, family gatherings include people you grew up with. The people you've done life with. You've experienced life (and sometimes death) with them. And that's why such gatherings are a more comfortable spot for somewhat challenging topics like religion and politics.

How does this transfer outside of familial relationships? Time, trust, and tact. It doesn't happen overnight, and it doesn't happen with ulterior motives in place. I'm talking about friendships that are enduring. I recognize that there is a spectrum. Some friends are the kind you'll want to retire with, go on family trips with, and celebrate every occasion with. Others are the kind you'll see for dinner every couple of months, but you pick up right where you left off. Still others you talk with once or twice a year, but there's a bond that exists despite time and distance. In other words, I'm not talking about people you just met at the playground or your kid's little league game. Sometimes opportunities will arise in those circumstances, but more often than not, that's just a chance to meet someone and set up a playdate.[11]

Ultimately, this is a book about relationships. Yes, you'll learn some about apologetics. Yes, you'll learn some about evangelism.

But more than anything, you'll learn about love. Because as Christians, we're called to love God and love people. Once we do those things well, it gets much easier to talk about our faith, share truth, and make disciples. After all, we should want to shout from the rooftops about the hope we have. This book will help you do that with confidence, grace, and love.

A NOTE ABOUT PEOPLE AND ORGANIZATIONS I MENTION IN THIS BOOK

Because this is a book about bridge building, I sought out sources from a wide variety of spaces, including some that are not often considered reliable or helpful by Christians. I understand why we are tentative about who we learn from, but I have found that we may miss noteworthy observations because we hold to differing theological or worldview perspectives. As such, I occasionally mention non-Christian people and organizations in this book. Please know this does not mean I endorse them. Although we may not always agree with non-Christians or professing Christians of certain backgrounds, there are certainly times when they make a point that can be informative, and it's for this reason that I include such points in this book.

PART 1

THE ART OF
BRIDGE BUILDING

Join together in following my example, brothers and
sisters, and just as you have us as a model, keep
your eyes on those who live as we do.

PHILIPPIANS 3:17

Don't burn bridges. You'll be surprised how many
times you have to cross the same river.[1]

H. JACKSON BROWN JR.

BUT FIRST, LET'S PRAY

*To be a Christian without prayer is no more
possible than to be alive without breathing.*

MARTIN LUTHER

You might be wondering why there's a chapter about prayer in a book about bridge-building apologetics. It is a fair question, and the answer is simple: Prayer is fundamental and foundational to our faith, to our relationship with the Father, and to our well-being as humans. I truly believe that you cannot have effective bridge building without prayer.

Did you know that prayer is beneficial to your health? Studies have shown that communal prayer (prayer with other people) can decrease levels of depression and anxiety.[1] Praying for others can decrease your anger and aggression,[2] as well as increase your desire to offer forgiveness.[3] In other words, you're more likely to be compassionate toward others (and even yourself) when you pray. You're more likely to engage in healthy conversations with others. And you're more likely to be well in your soul as well as your physical being. Prayer is a good thing.

Knowing this, perhaps you can see why we're talking about prayer in this book. But why is the chapter on prayer first, before we even talk about bridges or apologetics? That answer is simple too. We should pray before every time we share our faith, if possible. We should ask God for peace within the conversation, wisdom for the words to speak, and help with the recall of information. That's why I am beginning this book with a chapter about prayer. I believe that before we enter into conversations about our faith, we should pray. We should ask the Holy Spirit to join us in our endeavor. He is our helper, after all (we will talk more about this in chapter 15).

Prayer is a vital part of the Christian life. Don't leave home without it when you start to engage with others about your faith. I recognize that we have seasons when our prayer lives are vibrant and seasons when we can't think of a single word to say. I just had a friend tell me that she can do nothing but groan sometimes when her circumstances are utterly awful. Guess what? The Lord hears our groans too. He is compassionate toward His people (just look at the feeding of the 4,000 in Mark 8—Jesus knew the people were both spiritually and physically hungry, so He fed them spiritually and physically). My hope is that this chapter will help you develop an ongoing conversation with your Creator, the one who formed you in His image, the one who sent His only Son to save you. He wants to talk with you. You need only begin. The good news is that the more you talk with God, the easier it will be to share your relationship with Him with others.

Prayer is good for your spiritual health too. Not only does it bring you closer to your Creator, but it can also change your body and your mind, and it can impact the way you react toward others. In high school, I was a fan of contemporary Christian music artist Jaci Velasquez. One of her songs that sticks with me to this day is "On My Knees." As you may imagine from the title, it's a song about prayer—specifically, about how things change when we fall at the feet of Jesus. We're changed because our focus is re-centered on what matters—on who matters—when we pray. We're reminded that we are children of God, and we are loved deeply by Him. Praying can be difficult because it doesn't always seem natural, but we're meant to pray. Time and time again, Scripture exhorts us to pray:

- "Therefore I tell you, whatever you ask for in prayer, believe that you have received it, and it will be yours" (Mark 11:24).

- "Be joyful in hope, patient in affliction, faithful in prayer" (Romans 12:12).

- "Let your reasonableness be known to everyone. The Lord is at hand; do not be anxious about anything, but in everything by prayer and supplication with thanksgiving let your requests be made known to God. And the peace of God, which surpasses all understanding, will guard your hearts and your minds in Christ Jesus" (Philippians 4:5-7 ESV).

- "Is anyone among you suffering? Let him pray. Is anyone cheerful? Let him sing praise" (James 5:13 ESV).

Put another way, God commands us to pray. In his book *Prayer for Beginners*, Peter Kreeft explains, "We pray to obey God, not to 'play God.' We pray, not to change God's mind, but to change our own; not to command God, but to let God command us. We pray to let God be God."[4]

HOW DO WE BEGIN?

I read recently that singer and actor Meat Loaf (d. 2022) professed to be religious. When I dug a little deeper, I learned that he especially valued prayer. So much, in fact, that if he didn't pray, he apologized to God for the lack of communication with Him. With that in mind, it's worth remembering a few points: First, prayer is valuable. Second, we should be in constant prayer. And third, prayer is our way to be in conversation with our Father.

Prayer isn't meant to be used as a last resort when we can't find our car keys, although the attitude of dependence on God in times of need is one we should foster. How often do we let situations go completely south before thinking about asking the Lord for help? I'm guilty of this too. But the Bible tells us quite clearly that we should "pray continually" (1 Thessalonians 5:17). Easier said than done, though, right? And even when we want to heed this verse, we sometimes have no idea where to start. So, let's start where Jesus started—the Lord's Prayer.

Pray like Jesus

> This, then, is how you should pray:
> "Our Father in heaven,
> hallowed be your name,
> your kingdom come,
> your will be done
>   on earth as it is in heaven.
> Give us today our daily bread.
> And forgive us our debts,
>   as we also have forgiven our debtors.
> And lead us not into temptation,
> but deliver us from the evil one" (Matthew 6:9-13).

Not long ago, social media was ablaze because a question about the Lord's Prayer on the popular trivia show, *Jeopardy*, confounded all three contestants.[5] The news editor of *Christianity Today* called the situation "embarrassing,"[6] and others thought it confirmed a moral decline in our culture. Whether it's a sign of the times or not, I can't be sure, but I'm not surprised. In general, prayer is on the decline in both the US and the UK.[7] How can we expect anyone to know the words to arguably the most popular prayer in the world when prayer isn't a priority?

Early on in my service as a children's ministry director, I knew I wanted the children in my church to memorize the Lord's Prayer.

We often concluded our kids' services with the Lord's Prayer, including the ever-so-eloquent doxology "for thine is the kingdom, and the power, and the glory, forever and ever. Amen." I love hearing children pray, and I especially love it when we pray the Lord's Prayer together. Prayer is powerful when done in a community of believers. The Lord's Prayer was intended for community when Jesus taught it to His disciples. Reverend John Yieh summarizes it well:

> It reflects Jesus' concerns for God's holiness, God's kingdom, and God's will, and tells his followers which physical and spiritual needs they can ask God, their heavenly Father, to help meet. As a community prayer, it gives Christians identity, solidarity, and confidence as the beloved children of God. As a ritual practice, it strengthens the believers' filial relationship with God, sets priorities for their missions, and provides divine reassurance, inner peace, and eschatological hope to support their daily struggles with the contingencies of their lives and the evil in the world.[8]

In other words, the Lord's Prayer gives us the opportunity to focus on God and to truly give all of our thoughts, fears, and thanksgiving to Him, together with other believers. When you say this prayer, you're helping remind yourself that God is with you. He's for you. He's holy. And no matter what, He wants what is best for you. By saying the Lord's Prayer, you're telling the Father that you trust Him. That you need Him. And that no matter what, you'll serve Him. It's a great place to start when you don't know the words to say when you pray.

Scripture is full of examples of Jesus and His prayer habits. He prayed before performing miracles, to reveal His purposes, to deal with His own suffering and pain, and to ask for wisdom. He prayed alone and with others. In other words, He prayed without ceasing.

He was in constant conversation with the Father, and He gave us the example to follow in our own lives.

Memorizing and reciting the Lord's Prayer is a valuable spiritual practice, but there's a risk that it could become words we recite rather than a prayer we believe. Martin Luther once called the Lord's prayer "the greatest martyr on earth" because Christians don't use it properly—that is, with confidence in what it states.[9] James R. Nestingen explained that "the Lord's Prayer sees all of life *coram deo*, in relation to God; the neighbor is intimately involved in the hearing of God's word, the coming of the kingdom, and the doing of God's will."[10] *Coram deo* means to be or live in God's presence.[11]

So when you pray the Lord's Prayer, do so with confidence that you are in the presence of your Creator, the One who has the power to change your life and the lives of others. His name is hallowed and holy and to be revered with all you have within you. He equips you with all you need. The Lord's Prayer gives you an opportunity to remind yourself of God's greatness as well as His extraordinary love for you. What a blessing it is to know that we are in God's presence at all times, even when we feel alone. This is especially helpful to remember as bridge builders because it means we never enter a situation by ourselves—our wonderful and mighty Creator is with us.

Pray like Paul

> For this reason I kneel before the Father, from whom every family in heaven and on earth derives its name. I pray that out of his glorious riches he may strengthen you with power through his Spirit in your inner being, so that Christ may dwell in your hearts through faith. And I pray that you, being rooted and established in love, may have power, together with all the Lord's holy people, to grasp how wide and long and high and deep is the love of Christ, and to know this love that surpasses

knowledge—that you may be filled to the measure of all the fullness of God (Ephesians 3:14-19).

Ephesians 3 is its own gospel message. Paul was bold. He recognized God's power. He highlighted Jesus' love. If you've read Paul's letters in the New Testament, you've likely noticed that he liked to open with a greeting that included a prayer. For example, in Romans 1, he starts,

> First, I thank my God through Jesus Christ for all of you, because your faith is being reported all over the world. God, whom I serve in my spirit in preaching the gospel of his Son, is my witness how constantly I remember you in my prayers at all times; and I pray that now at last by God's will the way may be opened for me to come to you (verses 8-10).

Whew! Can you imagine saying that each time you write an email to a friend? But if you were to receive an email that opened with those words, how would you feel? We've already seen that praying for others can improve your sense of well-being, so maybe this is the way forward: a greeting with a reminder that we're praying for them.

A bridge builder like Paul knew what he was called to do: to share Jesus with others. He was called to spread the gospel far and wide, no matter the cost. And he found his strength in the Lord. He never left home without the Holy Spirit, and he always called on the Father when interacting with others. As Alister Begg explains, "Paul prayed big prayers because he believed great things."[12] He knew to pray with the expectation that God was ever present and all-powerful. Even in times of trial, Paul trusted that Jesus was who He said He was and could do what He said He could do. Ultimately, Paul believed the gospel. He knew it to be true, and he relied on its truth.

A major problem with the church as a collective is that people have lost sight of the gospel. Some who profess to be Christians don't even know the gospel message. A 2020 survey by the Cultural Research Center at Arizona Christian University found that 52 percent of the respondents who self-identified as Christians believe in a works-based salvation.[13] They aren't holding on to the hope within that comes from Christ alone, and they don't have sight of who they are as image bearers and children of God.

We, like Paul, should keep the gospel message at the center of our lives, not straying to the left or the right (Proverbs 4:27). Paul's reliance on the gospel was poured out in his prayer life, and he provides us with an excellent example of how to serve others by praying big.

Pray like the Psalmists

The past year has been difficult for me personally, and as I write this chapter, I'm dealing with some challenging circumstances in my life. I also just learned of yet another school shooting in which children and adults died needlessly at the hands of a gunman. I've been heartbroken due to loss, suffering, and the pain in our world. James 1:2-4 has echoed through my mind on an endless loop during this season: "Consider it pure joy, my brothers and sisters, whenever you face trials of many kinds, because you know that the testing of your faith produces perseverance. Let perseverance finish its work so that you may be mature and complete, not lacking anything." And I can't think of a better place to find examples of perseverance than in the Old Testament. Moses, David, Esther, Job, Ruth, and the Jewish people, just to name a few. We see evidence of their endurance in the Psalms.

- "Though he may stumble, he will not fall, for the LORD upholds him with his hand" (Psalm 37:24).

- "The LORD will vindicate me; your love, LORD, endures

forever—do not abandon the works of your hands" (Psalm 138:8).

- "God is our refuge and strength, an ever-present help in trouble. Therefore we will not fear, though the earth give way and the mountains fall into the heart of the sea, though its waters roar and foam and the mountains quake with their surging" (Psalm 46:1-3).

The Psalms are full of verses that are well suited to encouraging us to seek refuge in God when confronted with danger, whether that danger is physical or spiritual. As Eugene Peterson wrote in his book *Working the Angles*, "Everything that a person can possibly feel, experience, and say is brought into expression before God in the Psalms."[14] I've learned this firsthand. When I first started writing about world religions, I almost immediately had struggles spiritually.

For example, I have spent time studying the New Age movement, and as I got deeper into the trenches of it, I found myself feeling as though I was being weighed down. I felt like I was trudging through mud. I reached out to one of my mentors, Douglas Groothuis, and I asked him for help. I knew that he would have helpful advice because of his own experiences writing about the New Age movement. His recommendation? Pray Psalm 91. This psalm is often attributed to Moses, and he probably wrote it after he built the tabernacle. It's a prayer for protection and peace.

> Whoever dwells in the shelter of the Most High
>   will rest in the shadow of the Almighty.
> I will say of the LORD, "He is my refuge and my fortress,
>   my God, in whom I trust"…
> For he will command his angels concerning you
>   to guard you in all your ways;

they will lift you up in their hands,
   so that you will not strike your foot against a stone.
You will tread on the lion and the cobra;
   you will trample the great lion and the serpent
   (verses 1-2, 11-13).

This psalm reminds us that God is our refuge. Our fortress. He commands His angels on our behalf. The entire chapter is gold, and I highly encourage you to memorize it as you begin to engage with others about your faith.

Recently I tried a new practice during a devotional time with some of my co-workers. We all took Psalm 23 and rewrote it to apply to our own lives. The results were beautiful, and I was deeply encouraged to hear some of the different takeaways each of us gained from the same six verses. In my own reflection of Psalm 23, I found myself repeating, "The Lord is in control." This is a helpful practice if you are trying to engage with the book of Psalms in a new way, but remember that the takeaways you come up with are just that. Always be sure to read from the most reliable Bible translations and to correctly study and interpret the psalmists.

Another beautiful aspect of the Psalms is that they are mostly songs, which makes them perfect for easy memorization. The first time I memorized Psalm 91, I did so to music. My parents were missionaries, and singing was often how we memorized Scripture passages. Indeed, that's how the Jewish people likely memorized the Psalms too. After all, the word *psalm*, in Hebrew, means "to make jubilant music." With that in mind, there are musical versions of Psalm 91 available online. I encourage you to find one you like and memorize it. Then when you are faced with a spiritual battle, lean on the words as if they were a life raft in the middle of the ocean. Do not drown in your weariness. Instead, trust that God will deliver you.

You can put almost every psalm to music, so find one that resonates with you during this season of your life. Throughout the Psalms there are reminders of God's mercy, justice, and peace. Integrating the Psalms into your prayer life isn't difficult; take them one at a time. Elmer L. Towns, author of *Praying the Psalms*, says, "Each Psalm is a worship event...The Psalms are a mirror that reflects your soul."[15]

When you're bridge building, among the Psalms that you might find most helpful are Psalms 19, 57, 63, 122, 126, and 144. The following verses might be good starting points for you as you more openly share with others about the hope within you:

- "Teach me your way, LORD, that I may rely on your faithfulness; give me an undivided heart, that I may fear your name" (Psalm 86:11).

- "My mouth will speak words of wisdom; the meditation of my heart will give you understanding" (Psalm 49:3).

- "The LORD gives strength to his people; the LORD blesses his people with peace" (Psalm 29:11).

No matter where you begin in the Psalms, I do encourage you to begin. Take a psalm a day, and see how this practice can transform your prayer life, your view of the world, and your desire to share the gospel with others.

Pray like Leslie Strobel

You may know about Lee Strobel (author of books like *The Case for Christ* and *The Case for Miracles*), but perhaps you don't know much about his wife, Leslie. After she became a Christian, she was desperate to see Lee come to faith in Christ too, but it seemed like his heart was hardened. We all know that a hardened heart can be hard to penetrate. Lee says that Leslie's prayers were a key factor in his transformation and conversion to Christianity.[16]

Every day, Leslie prayed Ezekiel 36:26 on Lee's behalf: "I will give you a new heart and put a new spirit in you; I will remove from you your heart of stone and give you a heart of flesh." Maybe, like Leslie, you're engaging with someone who has a hardened heart toward God. Your words may seem to bounce off without sticking. But God's Word remains true. You are not alone—you have a helpmate, the Holy Spirit. Pray that God will produce the transformation that you cannot. God sees all and knows all and loves all. He wants to draw people to Himself. Allow your prayers to work on their behalf.

BUILDING THE BRIDGE

Prayer should be an important part of your Christian walk, especially as a bridge builder. If you're still wondering how to begin, let me remind you once more of how Jesus prayed and how He taught us to pray. He thanked His Father. He asked for comfort. He asked that people know God through the gospel. He even prayed for blessings before eating. If that's where you need to start, go for it. Pray before every meal, thanking God for His provision. Then make the move to praying for your loved ones, coworkers, and friends.

No matter where you begin, take that step because it will help you as you build bridges with others, and it will strengthen the bridge that you have been building toward God in your own life. In the context of bridge building, what should you be praying for? My top three go-tos are for peace, wisdom, and the presence of the Holy Spirit. Your top three might be different, but the ones I go with consistently help me through difficult or important conversations (like discussions about someone's eternal life).

Here are some starting points that might help you:

- Pray that your mind is protected from falsehood.

- Pray that God will give you the wisdom to know when to speak and when to listen.

- Pray that God will remind you of what you need to say to a particular person and what you can leave out.

- Pray that you'll have divine appointments and opportunities to share your faith.

- Pray that peace will be maintained throughout your conversations and afterward.

Ultimately, when we pray, we are reminded of the powerful God who created us and of His great love for us. Through prayer, transformation can happen, within us and in other people's lives. Andrew Murray summed it up beautifully in *The Prayer Life*: "Take time in the inner chamber to bow down and worship, and wait on Him until He unveils Himself and takes possession of you and goes out with you to show how a man may live and walk in abiding fellowship with an unseen Lord."[17] May your prayer life reveal Christ to others and strengthen your own faith in and love of the Father.

Whenever you are about to engage with a friend or acquaintance about your faith, take a deep breath first and say a prayer. When you hear a knock on your door, take a deep breath first and say a prayer. When you're asked about the hope that is within you, take a deep breath first and say a prayer.

QUESTIONS FOR REFLECTION AND DISCUSSION

1. What does the practice of prayer look like in your life right now?

2. How have you seen prayer make a difference in your life or in the life of someone you care about?

3. Do you think prayer brings you closer to God? Why or why not?

4. In what ways do you think prayer can help you sort through any anxiety you might feel when you attempt to build bridges and share your faith with others?

RECOMMENDED RESOURCES

Please be aware that the resources I recommend in this book may not always align with the Christian worldview or the faith tradition you believe. I've included books from all sides, including atheists. It's okay to read materials that challenge us and help us gain knowledge so that we may more effectively build bridges. I do not necessarily agree with everything found within the books and resources I recommend.

Chris Heinz, *Made to Pray: How to Find Your Best Prayer Types* (Bloomington, IN: WestBow Press, 2013)

Peter Kreeft, *Prayer for Beginners* (San Francisco, CA: Ignatius Press, 2000)

Tish Harrison Warren, *Prayer in the Night: For Those Who Work or Watch or Weep* (Downers Grove, IL: InterVarsity, 2021)

Alistair Begg, *Pray Big: Learn to Pray Like an Apostle* (Charlotte, NC: The Good Book Company, 2019)

Lectio 365 daily devotional app

2

EVERYTHING YOU NEED TO KNOW ABOUT BRIDGES
(UNLESS YOU'RE AN ENGINEER)

*I will not tell you how long or short the way will
be; only that it lies across a river. But do not fear
that, for I am the great Bridge Builder.*

**ASLAN, *THE VOYAGE OF THE DAWN TREADER*,
C.S. LEWIS**

One thousand feet in the air, and my heart was pounding. I didn't want to do it, but I knew that I needed to put on my big-girl pants and do it for the sake of our girls. The things we do for our kids, amiright?! They were nervous, but I knew this experience would be worth it. And as I put one tentative foot in front of the other, my nerves slowly subsided. When I looked down at my feet, I looked down into the great depths of the majestic Grand Canyon.

I put a lot of faith into the Skywalk that day. I'd done my homework beforehand, so I understood that it can hold 160,000 pounds without collapsing. It can also withstand an 8.0 earthquake, which is one of the most severe magnitudes on the Richter scale. Despite knowing these facts, I was still afraid. But then I looked over the railing and across the canyon. I was awestruck.

Here I was, seemingly walking on air above this beautiful masterpiece in creation. My fear morphed into relief as I stepped off the

37

see-through bridge and back into the building. But the inspiration didn't go away, so I willingly paid $35 to buy the keepsake photo—proof that our family had accomplished a grand feat together, simply by putting one foot in front of the other above the Grand Canyon.

Bridges can strike fear in the best of us. Some people even refuse to drive over bridges because they suffer from gephyrophobia—for them, this phobia can lead to severe panic attacks. If you've seen *The Middle* episode in which Brick tries to overcome his fear of crossing bridges, you know that it's not simple to overcome such a fear. His parents try to bribe him with money, ice cream, and more, but his terror of bridges could not be defeated. He was afraid that a bridge would collapse, and his family would die.

Others are afraid of bridges because some look sketchy and they even sway in the wind. Still others don't understand the mechanics of how bridges can handle the weight of the loads they carry. Sort of like some people who are afraid of flying—they wonder, *How does the plane stay in the air?* Regardless of why the fear exists, it's nearly impossible to avoid bridges. In the United States alone, there are more than 600,000 bridges.[1] They are everywhere.

Perhaps the same types of concerns arise when we think about sharing our faith with others. Opportunities are everywhere and endless, but often, we give in to fear and remain silent. In late 2021, Lifeway Research surveyed 1,002 Americans about evangelism. The good news is that 66 percent of respondents said they were open or very open to sharing their faith with a friend. Sixty-five percent of respondents said they are open or very open to talking with a friend about having a relationship with God. Only 13 percent said they were not open at all. Fifty-three percent said they were open or very open to talking with a stranger about having a relationship with God.

The bad news is that many of us aren't quite sure how to have the conversation. Twenty-four percent said they didn't know where to begin when sharing their faith, and 19 percent said they couldn't put the gospel message into words.[2] Even though the opportunity and openness are there, we don't understand the mechanics. Many of us are looking for a how-to manual to talk about God.

This is where bridge building comes in. Did you notice that more people in the Lifeway survey were willing to talk with their friends about faith than with strangers? Relationships open doors that otherwise wouldn't exist. This is probably why Thanksgiving gatherings can get rowdy—you're more likely to discuss religion and politics with people you know and love. This is true in all areas of life. Friends are more likely to help us move or to be a shoulder to cry on when it seems like the world is falling apart. This book is going to help you navigate the mechanics of bridge building so that you feel confident about sharing your faith when an opportunity arises.

WHAT'S A BRIDGE, ANYWAY?

Full disclosure: I'm not an engineer. The closest I have ever gotten to designing and constructing a bridge was in elementary school, when I built a bridge out of plumber's wire and heavyweight posterboard for the science fair. My dad (an actual engineer) helped me, and the bridge won first place because it held the weight it was supposed to hold without collapsing. Beyond that, my experience with building actual bridges is quite limited.

That said, I do know the purpose of bridges. They bring things together. Bridges connect landmasses, pieces of song, and even teeth. We find bridges on noses, electric circuits, and billiard cues. There's a card game called Bridge, the purpose of which is to have a successful partnership against another team. At my former church, we had a group for fifth and sixth graders called The Bridge because they are the bridge between young children and the youth group.

Bridges can help fill a void in a beautiful and sometimes unexpected way. For example, dental bridges replace a person's missing teeth, helping them to chew food better and improving their quality of life. Bridges in songs (also called the middle eight) sometimes give them the oomph they need to take it from good to great or great to even greater. Just listen to "Ain't No Mountain High Enough" or Toto's "Africa," and try to tell me that the songs would be better without the bridges found within them. People bridges, the kind of bridges we're working toward building, bring people together. Maybe it's people from different religions or different backgrounds or different political perspectives.

For the purposes of this book, I'll focus on bridges between landmasses because I think they provide the clearest similarities with people bridges. They come in a variety of shapes and sizes, and they have multiple purposes, though some have no purpose at all because they are literally bridges to nowhere.[3] Bridges are built using different means, like cables, trusses, and beams. Although bridges may appear unique and have various uses, civil engineer David Blockley says that all bridges between landmasses need three things to do their job well: a firm foundation, a strong structure, and effectiveness.[4] These apply to people bridge building, too, so it is useful to look at the three aspects and see how they apply to bridge-building apologetics.

A Firm Foundation

Foundations are important. Most people understand that if a structure doesn't have a firm foundation, it's more likely to topple down like a leaning tower of Jenga blocks. At the start of the COVID-19 pandemic, our neighborhood was in the midst of a growth spurt. My husband and I took walks daily and watched the progress as the new homes were being built. First, utilities were put into place and the ground was leveled—sometimes dirt was brought in, other times dirt was removed. Then the concrete foundation was laid. Not until after the foundation was cured (solidified) could the house be built on top of it. Otherwise, the house would eventually crumble. Nobody wants a house built on sinking sand, right? Read Matthew 7:24-27 to see what Jesus had to say about that (spoiler alert: it's not good).

Strong foundations are vital for bridges too. They must be able to hold not only the weight of the bridge itself but the loads that it carries. Not only must the foundation hold up the bridge; it must hold up everything that will be on the bridge. If the foundation fails, the bridge fails, and if the bridge fails, people could get injured or die.

Making sure the foundation is strong takes time and patience. Curing is the process that directly affects the strength and durability of whatever is built on the foundation. Have you ever driven through a construction zone on the highway and seen only a few or even no workers present? You may have thought, *Where are the workers?* It's possible they were waiting for the foundation to cure. The curing process is vital for success because literally everything rests on the stability of the foundation. It can take almost a month for the foundation of the bridge to cure, and that means waiting. If bridge builders get impatient and move too quickly, they put the stability of the bridge at risk.

Once a concrete bridge is built, the bridge deck needs time to cure too. The curing process for a bridge deck is a little different than for the concrete/soil that is cured underneath the ground. The bridge deck has to be cared for carefully; that is, it must be watered. Yes, as odd as that may sound, the concrete has to be watered so it will cure properly. It could take another week for the bridge deck to be strengthened to full capacity.

People bridges also require a firm foundation. We need to be patient and caring as we build bridges with others. Without taking time to allow for a curing process—that is, time for your foundation to become solid—it's possible that the foundation will not be secure. To avoid insecurity in a relationship, we should begin with a solid base. In fact, a firm foundation is so vital in bridge building that I've dedicated all of chapters 6 and 7 to the topic.

A Strong Structure

My daughter Thalia and I recently spent three days building a replica of the Golden Gate Bridge out of about 2,000 building blocks. We got frustrated at times because the pieces didn't always easily fit together, or we inadvertently skipped a step, which required us to go back and make a fix. Of course, our experience was significantly easier than the construction of the *actual* Golden Gate Bridge, which took more than four years to build. The bridge has withstood the test of time, too, from earthquakes to high winds to threat of collapse due to too many people on it. The foundation of the Golden Gate Bridge is sturdy, and as it nears its centennial anniversary, it continues to be an engineering marvel and a sight to behold. While we built the replica of the San Francisco landmark, Thalia and I learned that the structure of a bridge, even one made of building blocks, needs to be strong. Otherwise, the bridge will fail.

Bridges don't involve magic, though sometimes that seems to be the case when we look at them, doesn't it? There's a lot of technical genius and science that go into building bridges, involving things like tension, trusses, suspension, cables, beams, and arch supports. Bridge builders balance all of the force using compression and tension. Without a strong structure, bridges won't last very long—they'll collapse under the loads they carry. Engineers try to prevent bridge failures by including redundancy in their design and through periodic inspections for safety.[5]

When we are building bridges with people, we need to remember that we're not wizards waving wands and making others do what we say. Spells don't work. No, we are interacting with reality. We're speaking with humans who have value, perspective, emotions, and the capacity to reason. And just like with bridges, we should not use a one-size-fits-all approach to people. For example, some may require evidence before they're willing to believe the Bible is true. Others may look at nature and sense that God is real. Christianity is a strong structure on which to rely when interacting with others, so don't be afraid to throw all your weight into it. It won't collapse due to pressure.

An Effective Structure

Bridges are built to work. Otherwise, what's the point? Engineers follow rules and regulations to make the best bridges possible for any scenario. We don't build bridges expecting them to fail, and we build them to make access possible. For example, consider the Golden Gate Bridge. If it didn't exist, the roughly 15 million cars that cross it annually would have a much harder time getting between San Francisco and Marin County, California.[6] The same could be said of the 100,000 cars that cross the Brooklyn Bridge every day,[7] or the 59,000 cars that cross the Sunshine Skyway Bridge in Florida daily.[8] Bridges help people get to their destinations. They are good at what they are designed to do.

The same can be said for bridge building with people. We're called to be bold and loving: "If I speak in the tongues of men and of angels, but have not love, I am only a resounding gong or a clanging cymbal" (1 Corinthians 13:1). Resounding gongs aren't effective—they drown out everything else at their expense. Clanging cymbals aren't any better—they create useless noise. May the words that we speak be a balance of truth and love so that the bridges we build will be useful and effective.

A Structure That Unites

Bridges can be built in a number of ways—sometimes it's all about functionality (the current London Bridge, perhaps), and other times, the design is both functional and beautiful (for example, the Ruyi Bridge in China). One of the more interesting bridges I've seen is the Mathematical Bridge at Queens' College in Cambridge, the United Kingdom. Its fascinating design of crisscrossing wooden beams generates conversation amongst locals and tourists alike, and fun (albeit false) theories about its inception. The prevailing myth about the foot-bridge is that Sir Isaac Newton designed and built it using no nuts or bolts. Although a fun idea, the bridge was built long after Newton's death, and it does contain nuts and bolts—they are just cleverly disguised. Even so, the bridge is a good example of great design and structure.

Civil engineer Linda Figg notes that while bridges are functional, they also often serve as icons. "A bridge," she says, "can join riverbanks or cross great distances, but most profoundly it connects people to each other and to their dreams. A beautiful bridge can become an enduring symbol of an area, enabling and deepening a community's sense of itself."[9] Just like the Mathematical Bridge in Cambridge or the Brooklyn Bridge in New York or the Sydney Harbour Bridge in Australia. Even Waco, Texas, where I resided while penning this book, has a bridge that unites its community.

Let me give you another example. I grew up on the border of the United States and Mexico in Laredo, Texas. Each year, we celebrated George Washington's birthday with major pomp and circumstance, including parades, carnivals, and a city-wide ball. At one point during the celebration, there is an international bridge ceremony where four "Abrazo" (Spanish for hug) children meet in the middle of a bridge between Laredo and its sister city, Nuevo Laredo, Mexico. When they connect in the middle, the children exchange hugs as a sign of unity between the two cities. This has been happening since the early 1960s, and it's an absolutely lovely tradition, a rallying point for my hometown.

As bridge builders, we need to keep in mind that our desire is to connect, not divide. Yes, speak the truth. Bring darkness to light. But do so with respect and kindness. Bridges bring people together, not at the expense of truth, but as a sign of love and compassion.

This isn't to say that there will never be division. Indeed, Jesus said that He came to "bring fire on the earth" as well as "division" (Luke

12:49-51). Not everyone will want to learn about Him or talk with you. There will be times when you'll need to put up boundaries and barriers (see chapter 13). We can still do our best, though, to bring peace. After all, Jesus is still the Prince of Peace (Isaiah 9:6).

SOMETIMES BRIDGES FAIL— BUT IT'S NOT INEVITABLE

You might have seen video footage of the Tacoma Narrows Bridge in Washington twisting and eventually collapsing in 1940 due to high winds—no people died that day, but a dog named Tubby did.[10] On August 1, 2007, a bridge in Minneapolis collapsed in the middle of rush hour. More than 100 vehicles tumbled into the Mississippi River. Thirteen people died, and dozens of others were injured. On October 30, 2022, the cables snapped on a 120-year-old suspension bridge in Morbi, India, killing 141 people, including more than 50 children, and injuring almost 200 others. The worst bridge tragedy in history, though, happened in Portugal in 1809, during the Peninsular War. Approximately 4,000 people died when the overloaded Ponte das Barcas bridge collapsed.

Sometimes bridges fail.[11] They fail for many reasons, ranging from age, design or manufacturing defects, and poor maintenance to natural disasters like floods and earthquakes. About 7 percent of the bridges in the United States are "structurally deficient"—that is, they need a lot of maintenance, or the likely result will be catastrophic.[12] I'm not telling you this so that you approach bridges with fear. In fact, you might find it comforting that this is a significant improvement from just a couple of decades ago, when more than 25 percent of bridges were structurally deficient.[13] Yet bridges continue to age and deteriorate faster than we can fix them.

I don't want this to be the image of Christianity or apologetics, that we're deteriorating faster than we can be repaired. I've heard too many stories about how people were harmed by the church or Christians. The typical excuse given is that Christians are people, and people fail. People mess up. People destroy. Instead of looking at people, we're told by fellow Christians or church leaders that we should consider Christ. Yes and no. It is a cop-out to blame our failure on our humanity.

Broken Bridges Can Be Rebuilt (or Recycled)

The various Departments of Transportation throughout the United States are responsible for maintaining and repairing more than 617,000 bridges nationwide.[14] I've got good news and bad news about bridge repair. The bad news is that it seems we learn best when there is a catastrophe. For example, a bridge in Philadelphia collapsed in June 2023 when a fiery crash underneath it softened the steel that held it up. This tells engineers that when they build new bridges, they need to use fireproof or at least fire-resistant materials. The good news is that with improved technology, the outlook is promising. In the case of the danger of melting steel, fire insulation is possible, albeit somewhat impractical because there are thousands of steel bridges in the US. One civil engineer, Nur Yazdani, has a simple suggestion: start where it matters most—"energy corridors."[15] By focusing on where the need presents itself most, we will see the most productive results.

The same can be said of bridge building with people. Don't cut your losses and quit when you see how many bridges need repair and restoration (it doesn't take much investigation to see the damage left in the wake of various church scandals and careless Christians). Instead, see where your gifts and friendship and love can be best used right now. Try to build and restore what you can and pray that others will do the same. Though you are only one person, every little bit helps.

Despite our best efforts, bridges may still fall down. We should do what we can to salvage what we can of a relationship that may have been hurt. We can look to the example of companies that use the broken concrete from capsized bridges to restore life in the ocean. "Concrete that cannot be recycled is barged out to the ocean and left to create an artificial reef," Figg explains. "Reefs strengthen fishing economies and help regenerate underwater ecology. The recycling gives the old bridge a new life."[16] In other words, not all is lost when a bridge collapses or is torn down.

Of course, we are human. We are fallen, and we make mistakes. People have been hurt by Christians and churches, all in the name of Christ and our Creator. Christianity rides or dies on the cross and Jesus' resurrection and role as our Savior. So, if we know of bridges in our lives that need repair, we should pay attention to them before they collapse. Yes, sometimes our mistakes lead our bridges to crumble or fail, but Christ can help us to pick up those pieces. He won't fail. That is why we are the church of hope.

One Last Thing About Bridges...

Bridges aren't tunnels. Unlike tunnels, bridges aren't underground or hidden. Bridges can be seen. Tunnels plow through terrain while bridges are built across or above. And let's face it: bridges are usually less claustrophobic than tunnels. As Christians, we don't want to keep the gospel hidden, and we certainly don't want people to feel steamrolled or suffocated when they're talking with us. Let's strive to build bridges, not tunnels.

BUILDING THE BRIDGE

Building bridges to others could be considered a skill, but we should view it as a calling. Some of us may be more gifted in doing this than others, but that doesn't give anyone a free pass to avoid bridge building. As you'll discover in the rest of this book, bridges that are built with a firm foundation and a strong structure are the most effective (just like the bridges we cross every day). Sometimes we may discover cracks that need repairing, but again, that doesn't give us an excuse to step away from the call. With the Lord's wisdom and guidance, building bridges to people can be a rewarding experience that benefits everyone involved. And when we add the gospel and apologetics, we open the door to sharing our faith in ways that could transform a life or two.

Ultimately, I hope this book will enable you to feel confident that you can have effective conversations about your faith without being fearful or a jerk. And before we dive into some lessons about how to build bridges with people in mind, let's cover some important basics about apologetics.

QUESTIONS FOR REFLECTION AND DISCUSSION

1. Have you ever been afraid to cross a bridge? How did you overcome your fear?

2. What's the most amazing bridge you've ever seen? Why were you so impressed with it?

3. What is one way you can ensure that your bridges with people have a firm foundation?

4. A strong structure is necessary for effective bridges. What does this mean for people bridges?

5. How can we work to repair the bridges that need mending in our lives?

RECOMMENDED RESOURCES

Practical Engineering, YouTube channel

Judith Dupré, *Bridges: A History of the World's Most Spectacular Spans* (New York: Black Dog & Leventhal Publishers, 2017)

Charles A. Whitney, *Bridges of the World: Their Design and Construction* (Mineola, NY: Dover Publications, 2003)

3

APOLOGETICS—A BRIDGE IN NEED OF REPAIR?

The gospel is what saves, and apologetics is the servant of the gospel message.[1]

MATT SLICK

It's possible you're reading this book and you've never heard of apologetics before now. If so, I'm so glad you took a step of faith and still took a chance on the book, even if you didn't fully understand what you were getting into. And if you *have* heard of apologetics before, it's possible that you've never been given a clear definition of it. One of the most common questions I get about apologetics is, "Why are you apologizing for your faith?" So, let's clear the air from the start: *Apologetics is not apologizing for your faith.* Another fact you should know from the start is that not all apologists are Christians. Or argumentative. Or jerks. And that's one of the reasons I wrote this book.

I came to faith at a young age. My parents were missionaries, and my dad is a pastor. My faith was good enough for me until it wasn't, until I realized that it wasn't good enough for those around me, for those I loved the most. Or at all (newsflash: we're called to love our neighbors, and, well, that includes pretty much everyone). Part of loving my neighbors well includes being able to give a reason for the hope within me whenever they ask (1 Peter 3:15).

I wasn't really exposed to apologetics until college, and at that point, I didn't have a name for it. I just thought I was doing comparative religions by researching different worldviews and evaluating their truth claims. I didn't do a deep dive then, but I read Fritz Ridenour's book *So What's the Difference?* and that helped clarify some of the distinctions between the different worldviews I encountered daily.[2]

My next encounter with apologetics happened about five years later when my then boyfriend, now husband, Jay, became a Christian. He did a deep dive of his own in college to investigate his beliefs, and at the end of it, he gave his life to Christ. He hasn't stopped pursuing truth, and he continues to push me theologically and intellectually to know why I believe what I do. Back then, I was grateful for his personal pursuit and ultimate conversion, but I still didn't see why I needed to know arguments for the faith. I didn't like to debate with people, even though I was an attorney. You see how I thought being an apologist meant arguing with people? I just wanted others to know that the Bible is true, not argue with them about it.

Then Jay went to seminary. We discovered a discount for spouses, and I decided it was as good a time as any for me to fully consider the truth claims of Christianity. Plus, I wanted to understand so many of the things he was so excited about (because, let's be honest, when you hear the phrase *Kalam cosmological argument*, your stomach drops a little). So, I enrolled in the apologetics and ethics program at Denver Seminary, and that's when things changed for me. That's when my faith transitioned from being ethereal to tangible, something that I could defend and grasp on to. That's when I had the aha moment I talked about in the introduction.

APOLOGIA = DEFENSE

It turns out that apologetics is defending what you believe. The word *apologetics* is derived from the Greek word *apologia*, which means "to give a defense." It's the same term used to describe what happens in a court of law. Questions are asked, and answers are given (unless someone wants to be held in contempt). And being able to answer questions about what you believe matters, especially in this day and age. Conviction matters.

As a mom and through my experiences as a children's ministry director, it has become even more important for me to be able to answer my children's questions about Christianity. And they keep me on my toes. Kids really do ask some of the wildest questions—questions like these:

- "How much poop was on Noah's ark?"

- "Why did Ruth steal Boaz's blanket? Didn't she think he might be cold?"

- "How can God be three people in one?"

The more I talk with people, the more I realize that it's not just kids who are desperate for answers. As culture shifts (we seem to see some kind of cultural shift every generation), people seem hungrier to learn about worldview and faith. And that's where apologetics comes in—not to save the day but to offer help, and not just for others, but for you too. The more you equip yourself now, the better you'll be able to respond to your own doubts should any creep in later.

APOLOGISTS HAVE A REPUTATION
(AND IT'S NOT ALL SUNSHINE AND RAINBOWS)

I came into the world of apologetics not knowing much about it, but I quickly realized that it has a bit of a bad reputation. Just ask people on X (formerly Twitter)—they'll tell you all about it, I'm sure. And I wouldn't be surprised if you have some preconceived notions about Christian apologists. Trust me, I've been there. It's true that there seem to be some issues in the foundation and structure of apologetics that absolutely affect the effectiveness of apologists. There are ways that doing apologetics needs repair, from ensuring the evidence we present is sound to watching the ways we engage with unbelievers as well as with fellow Christians. If we aren't willing to see the ways we can fix what is broken, bridge building will be impossible.

That said, not every criticism stated about apologists or apologetics is true. Some of the claims or assumptions you've heard or read may, in fact, be false. Consequently, I'd like to address some common myths and misconceptions about apologetics and apologists.

Myth #1: Apologetics Is Only for Christians

Apologetics is the practice of defending your worldview (which is a beefy word but simply refers to how people view the world—like, why we exist, or what God's role is in our lives, or whether babies should get baptized). There are Christian apologists, Muslim apologists, Latter-day Saint apologists, and even atheist apologists (though I've learned over time that atheists often don't like to be called apologists). You are an apologist for your worldview, whatever it may be. Maybe you're not offering a verbal defense for what you believe, but your life is an apologetic for what you believe. Either way, what you say and do tells people your worldview. As a Christian, you want to be sure to speak the truth with your words and show the truth with your deeds.

And why should Christians consider apologetics? Because doing so will, at the very least, cause you to examine the reasons you believe what you do. Everyone should do that. Why do you believe Christianity is true? Is it because you had an emotional experience (and it's okay if that is the case)? Did you come to Jesus because you're convinced that the resurrection truly occurred? Maybe it was because you looked at nature and said, "That couldn't have happened on its own."

However you came to faith, it is important to examine the Christian truth claims for yourself so that you can be prepared to defend your hope if someone asks about it. You wouldn't show up in court without evidence, would you? The same goes for our faith.

Myth #2: Apologists Need to Know a Lot About a Lot

Not quite. I'll admit that some of the best apologists have advanced degrees, but they aren't experts in everything. Just because someone is an expert in one field does not make them an expert in all fields. It works better when we stay in our own lanes, but sometimes it's tempting to dabble and explore other areas. In other words, use the gifts God has given you (including your specific passions) to determine your apologetics interests, and support others in their areas of interest.

What's amazing about apologetics is its vastness. Whether you're interested in philosophy or history or science, there's something for you. For example, William Lane Craig speaks and writes primarily about philosophy. Holly Ordway emphasizes the Christian imagination and apologetics, using her expertise in English as a guide. Hugh Ross and Sarah Salviander, both astrophysicists, engage mostly with issues involving science. Biochemist Fazale Rana talks a lot about science and finding common ground between different views. My husband, Jay, specializes in psychological apologetics. There are other apologists defending the Christian worldview in their own fields of study. You'll find it helpful to keep a list of people you can recommend if someone asks you a question outside of your expertise.

Myth #3: All Apologists Are Jerks

Nope. In fact, I would venture to say that most of us are not jerks. Unfortunately, what you see on social media and even in real life from time to time might tell you differently. I've seen it myself. A well-meaning person asks a question about the Christian church or theology or politics or sexuality, and some not-so-well-meaning

Christians pounce, ready to attack. Maybe they don't want to attack the question asker, but instead, they pounce on those trying to answer the question. An argument ensues, and everyone leaves the conversation with a bad taste in their mouth. Worse, the outcome might turn the original question asker against Jesus because Christians engaged with hostility rather than respect. Don't be a jerk for Jesus.

Maybe you grew up in the 1970s and 1980s, and your exposure to apologetics left you feeling as though you were on trial for murder and the prosecutor was gung-ho not to let you get a word in during cross-examination. Instead, they ask questions to prove a point, not hear your perspective. They are not interested in hearing information; rather, they want to give it. This sometimes happens when Latter-day Saint or Jehovah's Witness missionaries show up at a Christian's door.[3] The Christian may have prepared for this moment—not to hear what the missionaries have to say, but to respond to what they *think* the missionaries will say. This isn't the best way to make a great first impression. Worse yet, it makes the Christian appear as a know-it-all who doesn't care to listen to someone else's perspective. *Don't be a jerk for Jesus.*

First Peter 3:15 says, "In your hearts revere Christ as Lord. Always be prepared to give an answer to everyone who asks you to give the reason for the hope that you have. But do this with gentleness and respect." I fear that many of us have forgotten that last part, and that's one of the reasons I felt so compelled to write this book. Gentleness and respect are key parts of defending our faith. At least they should be. We shouldn't destroy people (2 Corinthians 10:5). It is so easy to point out examples of Christians behaving badly on social media or in the world around us, but take some time to notice the good examples too.

One such example happened in 2020, when the former frontman of the Christian band Hawk Nelson deconstructed from Christianity. Jon Steingard publicly announced his deconversion on a since-deleted Instagram post, saying, "After growing up in a Christian home, being a pastor's kid, playing and singing in a Christian band, and having the word 'Christian' in front of most of the things in my life—I am now finding that I no longer believe in God." Jon's deconversion resulted in many bloggers and podcasters commenting about him, including a blog post from Christian apologist Erik Manning. In his blog,[4] Erik called out Jon directly, and Jon caught wind of the post. This prompted him to tweet, "Thanks for triggering a wave of love and support for me tonight. It was timely and encouraging. I hope some of those good vibes make it back to you as well."[5]

Erik replied the next day. Instead of defending his blog post, he apologized and said,

> Hi Jon. I wrote this and regret doing it. I don't disagree with 100% of what I said, but I disagree with a good part of it and ESPECIALLY using your name as a platform to preach. It was shallow of me. I'd be happy to talk things over with you privately. I've asked [Cross Examined] to remove it.

Jon, apparently touched by Erik's reply, reacted graciously and said,

> This is brave and kind Erik. I actually didn't feel wronged by what you wrote. I wrote about my changing views publicly, so others also writing publicly felt like fair game. I too would write my Instagram post very differently if I wrote it today. We never stop growing right?

The conversation ended with Erik's answer:

> I don't know the full scope of your deconversion story and what you went through, and I wanna take this as an opportunity to learn to be quick to listen and slow to speak.

As you can see, apologists, just like anyone else, are going to make mistakes. But many, like Erik, will own up to their error and apologize. He humbled himself, and he asked for forgiveness. Does it happen every time? No. As Jon said, "We never stop growing."

There are countless other examples online and in real life of apologists who treat others with respect, even when they disagree on things.[6] All that to say, not all apologists are jerks. Yes, there are some bad seeds. Yes, mistakes have been made. But we shouldn't allow a few bad examples to poison the entire well. Instead, we should call out wrong behavior and strive to be different. In other words, don't be a jerk for Jesus.

Myth #4: Apologists Don't Know How to Listen

I've already alluded to this myth earlier, but truly, not listening well is a big problem when it comes to evangelism or sharing the good news. I've found that a lot of times, even when we have the best intentions, we are so preoccupied with how to counter the claims we hear that we don't take the time to truly listen to what's being said. Don't focus solely on your next point when you're talking with someone about religion (or anything else). Instead, listen well. Then ask questions.

We should take a page out of theologian Francis Schaeffer's experience: "If I have only an hour with someone, I will spend the first fifty-five minutes asking questions and finding out what is troubling their heart and mind, and then in the last five minutes I will share something of the truth."[7] I've heard it said in a simpler way: *Sit in the grass with them.* In other words, find a space where you can relax with someone and have a friendly chat. We'll talk about this more throughout this book.

Myth #5: Apologists Just Want to Fight and Be Right

Are you starting to see some trends here? All of these negatives tend to go hand in hand. If you listen well and allow others to share their perspectives, it is unlikely they will call you a jerk for Jesus. I have seen many battles on social media that would seem to prove this myth. And the fighting isn't just with atheists or people who hold to other worldviews. It's with other Christians. Don't believe me? Look for discussions between Christians about baptism, eschatology (the end times), modesty, female roles in the church, or creation.

I'm sure that most Christians enter the fray with unbelievers with good intentions—to share the gospel and point people to Jesus. Unfortunately, for far too long, we've been told that we're engaging in a war, so we turn each conversation into a battle.

Although it may seem like every apologist wages war with anyone who holds to a different worldview, that's not true. Most apologists realize they are in a spiritual battle, not one of flesh and blood (see Ephesians 6:12). I'll admit that sometimes Christian apologists get carried away by their passion for the gospel, and sometimes, the exchange gets heated or out of hand. But not all apologists engage in that kind of behavior.

As for being right all the time, I would venture to guess that most people want to be right about everything they think or believe. We don't go out into the world thinking, *What can I be wrong about today?* I think the reason things sometimes go haywire is because we (I'm talking the collective *we* here, not just apologists) are unwilling to admit we're wrong. In short, we're prideful. But that's not a biblical attitude—"pride goes before destruction, a haughty spirit before a fall" (Proverbs 16:18).

My fellow Mama Bear, Hillary, often reminds our podcast listeners that we're probably not right about everything, and one day in eternity, God Himself will fill us in on our mistakes. May we never be so buried under our pride that we miss the truth. May we be humble enough to admit when we've gotten something wrong so that we don't lead others astray. Will some Christian apologists mess up? Absolutely. But we should hope that rarely happens.

BUILDING THE BRIDGE

Nobody is perfect, and apologists certainly aren't. We're human. Most of us, though, desire to do the best we can to share truth and point people to Christ. Our humanness sometimes becomes a stumbling block, whether due to pride or lack of empathy or simply a desire to be right (we engage with others because we believe wholeheartedly that what we're saying is not only true but has eternal consequences).

As we build bridges to others, we need to remember to speak with courage, compassion, and clarity. We muddy the waters and shift away from the gospel when we forget that we are called to make disciples. For us to forget the call, or the purpose behind what we do, takes us away from God's glory and into our own. Therefore, bridge building requires humility, kindness, and an ability to see people as they are—people made in God's image and with whom God desires an eternal relationship. In the next chapter, we will connect the dots between bridge building and apologetics so that we can engage effectively without accidentally causing rifts that are beyond repair.

QUESTIONS FOR REFLECTION AND DISCUSSION

1. How would you describe apologetics to someone who had never heard the word before?

2. What convinces you that your worldview is true?

3. Challenge yourself: Present the gospel message in 30 seconds.

4. How can Christians help repair some of the damage that has been done that has sullied the reputation of believers, and worse, of our Savior?

5. What are some preconceived notions you've had about apologetics or apologists?

RECOMMENDED RESOURCES

C.S. Lewis, *Mere Christianity*, rev. ed. (San Francisco, CA: HarperOne, 2015)

Charles E. Moore, *Called to Community: The Life Jesus Wants for His People* (Walden, NY: Plough Publishing, 2016)

Norman Geisler and Jason Jimenez, *The Bible's Answers to 100 of Life's Biggest Questions* (Ada, MI: Baker, 2015)

Richard Swinburne, *Is There a God?*, rev. ed. (Oxford: Oxford University Press, 2010)

Gordon Fee, *How to Read the Bible for All Its Worth* (Grand Rapids, MI: Zondervan, 2014)

4

BRIDGES + APOLOGETICS = BRIDGE–BUILDING APOLOGETICS

Blind faith turns out, therefore, to be the exact opposite of the biblical one.

JOHN LENNOX

Now that we have a clearer idea of bridges and apologetics, let's put them together. Bridge-building apologetics is about connecting with others the way Jesus did. We need to start with a firm foundation and strong structure so we can be effective. We might find some bridges in need of repair and restoration. We might stumble upon some heaps of rubble that used to be bridges. The work may be messy. But on the other side, we hope to end up better humans and better Christ-followers because of the effort put into relationships and loving our neighbors as ourselves.

Bridge builders don't manipulate people. Keep in mind what Paul told the Roman Christians:

> I urge you, brothers and sisters, to watch out for those who cause divisions and put obstacles in your way that are contrary to the teaching you have learned. Keep away from them. For such people are not serving our Lord Christ,

but their own appetites. By smooth talk and flattery they
deceive the minds of naive people (Romans 16:17-18).

In other words, check your intentions. What are you trying to do
with bridge building? Manipulative people set out to exert power over
others for selfish purposes. That's not bridge building. In fact, that's
the opposite of what we are called to do as Christians. Bridge builders resolve conflicts. They create relationships. With that in mind,
bridge-building apologetics is entering into a relationship with the
other person's outcome in mind, not your own. If you enter a relationship with ulterior motives, you've missed the point.

CREATE RELATIONSHIPS

One of the things that strikes me the most about Jesus is His desire
to be in relationship with His disciples and others. He clearly had a
good relationship with His mother and her friends—He and the disciples even attended a wedding with Mary (this is when He changed
water to wine, in John 2:1-10). He also seemed to have gotten along
well with His cousin John (the Baptist) as well as Lazarus (for whom
He wept in John 11:35). In other words, Jesus knew He needed people in His life, people who would encourage Him and support Him.

When Jesus called His disciples, often He would simply ask them
to join Him, as done with Matthew (see Matthew 9:9) or with Andrew
and Peter (see Matthew 4:18-20). Once the disciples joined Jesus' team,
so to speak, they spent a lot of time together. Think about when you
hang out with your friends. You laugh, you eat together, you sometimes get sillier than normal. These men were with Jesus for three
years. Of course they were accomplishing the mission of establishing God's kingdom, but they were also friends. They were probably
a lot like family by the time Jesus was crucified. They experienced
losses together and went through trials together. They traveled long

distances with one another. They prayed together. They were in relationship with one another. And it seems like even though Jesus knew He would be with them for only a short time, His relationship with them was a priority. So it should be with us.

I moved a lot as a kid, and often I would wonder if we were going to move again after we had been in one place for a while. There were times when I didn't want to make friends because I didn't want to end up leaving friends behind. In adulthood, I eventually learned to value the time I had with people, even if it was a short while. This became especially important after my husband and I got married because he was in the US Air Force. I knew we would be stationed in any one place for only a few years at a time, and we needed to make those years count. And even though he's no longer on active duty, we have still had to move a few times during the last ten years. Even so, we have gotten better at building meaningful relationships with others over time. And the goodbyes have gotten harder with each move, which for me is a sign that the relationships have grown deeper.

Developing relationships can be daunting, especially when you're in a situation where you don't know anyone. This is one reason why I've included an entire chapter about friendships. I truly believe that genuine friendships are a foundation to bridge building. Bonds can be formed through highs and lows. Maybe it's seeing the same neighbors at the gas station every week or getting to know other parents at the PTA. Maybe it's an unexpected storm that brings you together.

Shortly before we moved away from Waco, Texas, we experienced the worst hailstorm I've ever seen. The hail was the size of baseballs—and Waco made national news. Every home in our neighborhood was hit, and as the clouds rolled away, people slowly came out of their homes to survey the damage. Car windows were busted up and down our streets. Windows on homes were destroyed. Every roof had to be replaced. No home was unscathed. And then another storm rolled in. Neighbors jumped into action helping each other put tarps on cars so that the incoming rain wouldn't cause more damage. And guess what? That storm experience will forever be shared between neighbors. Some of us learned each other's names for the first time. Some started trusting their neighbors for the first time. We were changed because of the weather.

Whether it's a storm or a PTA meeting, see your encounters with other people as opportunities to create relationships because, as psychiatrist Bruce Perry said, "Relationships matter: the currency for systemic change was trust, and trust comes through forming healthy working relationships. People, not programs, change people."[1] People change other people. We are changed by others, and they are changed by us. And the bricks we lay in the course of bridge building must be bonded by the mortar of our relationship with Jesus Christ.

Laying the First Brick

As we learned earlier, bridges require a firm foundation. And in the context of bridge building with people, the two essentials for a firm foundation are truth and friendship, which we will address in chapters 8 and 9. But what about the bricks we are laying to build an effective bridge? Well, those bricks are all the things that happen in relationships—from first impressions to dying breaths to everything in between.

The first brick is your first interaction. In their book *First Impressions*, Nalini Ambady and John J. Skowronski suggest that first impressions are "absolutely fundamental to the processes of person perception and social cognition."[2] In other words, our first impressions impact the way we see people and how they see us, and not just in the short term, but in the long term. First impressions leave permanent marks.

> Expectations derived from first impressions can lead to biases in processing as well as self-fulfilling prophecies. Moreover, inaccurate or biased first impressions may

have serious implications for later affect, cognition, and behavior. More specifically, the first impression that may seem fleeting now may actually persist in an individual's mental representation of others.[3]

What we do in those first moments leaves an impact, and our attitudes can influence the long-term outcomes of a potential relationship. Former FBI negotiator Chris Voss explains that "when we radiate warmth and acceptance, conversations just seem to flow. When we enter a room with a level of comfort and enthusiasm, we attract people toward us."[4]

The good news is that although it may be difficult to overcome a bad first impression, it is not impossible.[5] Interestingly, overcoming one may have a lot to do with your morality.[6] It sort of reminds me of the old Blockbuster Video store slogan, "Be kind and rewind." If you want to override a poor first interaction with someone, admit the error (if there was an error) and let them know you'd like to try again. Show kindness and humility in the moment. They may reject your offer, but if they observe consistency in your positive behavior, they are more likely to change their mind. It certainly wouldn't hurt to give it your best shot. Every time you interact with others, you're leaving seeds. Those seeds may sprout, or they may not. Sometimes that will be due to something you said or did (intentionally or not), and sometimes it has nothing to do with you at all.

Sowers of Seeds

The first time Jesus taught a parable, He spoke to a crowd in Galilee about sowing seeds (Matthew 13). At this point in His ministry, He was facing more and more opposition among the people, and He saw this as an opportunity to share about the acceptance and rejection of His message. When we are in relationships with people, we need to understand that what we do and say matters, not just in a first-impression sense, but in an eternity sense. We must always be kingdom minded, even if we don't talk about our faith directly. Jesus was teaching the Galileans about seeds to encourage them despite the growing dissension toward His message.

Jesus began His teaching with a parable about a sower, a person who plants seeds. He then explained what happened next: The seeds scattered on the path were eaten by birds; the seeds scattered on the rocks didn't take root, so the sun burned them up; the seeds in the thorns got swallowed by the thorns; and the seeds on the good soil flourished (verses 3-8). He concluded with "He who has ears, let him hear" (verse 9). We'll get back to that in a minute.

New Testament scholar Craig Blomberg explains that this parable would have made sense to the crowd because they understood "broadcast sowing—scattering seeds in all directions by hand as they walked up and down the stony paths that divided their fields."[7] Jesus was speaking with clarity because He wanted His listeners to understand His words. Yet the disciples seemed confused by Jesus' use of parables (see verse 10). He was likely speaking to them privately at this point, not in front of the crowd. Admittedly, His answer is a little confusing. Blomberg suggests that "Jesus' reply points to the two-pronged purpose of parables—to reveal and to conceal."[8] God's timing was everything. Some would understand immediately, and others would not. Those who were meant to hear and understand would. This harkens back to Matthew 5:3, when Jesus said, "Blessed are the poor in spirit, for theirs is the kingdom of heaven." We're nothing without Christ, and by admitting that, we are able to see His message and grasp the meaning: The kingdom of heaven is near, so let's be heavenly minded.

Jesus (perhaps because He's all-knowing and He knew that the people needed an explanation) took some time to expound on the parable of the sower. Not everyone who hears the Word will understand it. Blomberg notes, "The parable provides a sober reminder that even the most enthusiastic outward response to the gospel offers no guarantee that one is a true disciple."[9] Indeed, Jesus discussed weeds (verses 24-30), which appear similar to wheat but destroy rather than sustain. Ultimately, Jesus brought it all together by declaring Himself the farmer (verse 37). He ended His lesson with a question: "Have you understood all these things?" (verse 51). He was preparing His followers to lay the seeds of truth to prepare the way for the kingdom of heaven. That's the mission of every bridge builder, whether done explicitly in conversations about faith or implicitly in the way we portray the character of our Savior.

WHAT ARE YOU SOWING?

Unfortunately, and maybe unsurprisingly, Bible reading is down in the US. The American Bible Society's 2022 *State of the Bible* survey indicates a decline in the number of Americans who engage with Scripture outside of church services—four in ten say they never do. Only about 10 percent of Americans say they read their Bible every day.[10] How can we know what the Bible says if we don't read it?

Anecdotally, I've noticed that very few church attendees bring their own Bibles (and of those who do, many use a Bible app rather than a printed version). So many people seem to rely on what the preacher says. Don't do this. One of the best ways to know whether you're being taught correctly at church is to check Scripture yourself as your pastor teaches. Check the context. Double-check the words. And then read your Bible at home. Doing this has been made simpler with Bible apps and read-aloud versions. Daily Scripture reading will help you in several ways:

1. Equip you to answer tough questions and do good works (2 Timothy 3:16-17)

2. Encourage and convict you (Hebrews 4:12)

3. Remind you that you're not fighting spiritual battles alone
   (2 Corinthians 10:3-6)

4. Reveal truth (John 17:14-17)

How can you sow seeds of truth if you don't know truth? Truth comes from the Bible and from God's creation. We do not find truth in what the world proclaims as truth if it is contrary to Scripture. With that in mind, how's your Bible reading practice? Can you spot truth from nontruth when it comes to the Word? It's common knowledge that FBI agents who specialize in detecting counterfeit money study real money so that they can easily spot the fake when it comes across their desk. Would you be able to spot the fake if it came across yours? The best way we can prepare ourselves to sow seeds of truth is to know the truth. We can't know the truth if we do not read it.

ADD IN SOME COLOR

In addition to diving into Scripture, I want to encourage you to read books and listen to podcasts about apologetics. Look first for information experts—people who have studied in their fields and have credibility among their peers. Start with primary sources, and then if you'd like to learn more, read books written about the primary sources or about specific topics of interest. The more you research specific topics and fields, the better prepared you'll be when you engage in relationships with others. And the more comfortable you'll be building bridges. Apologetics is as much for you as it is for the people you share with. You will equip yourself with truth so that in times of doubt (which are completely normal), you'll know where to go to reinforce the truths you've already learned.

LAYING THE REST OF THE BRICKS

Once you've established a relationship, the real fun begins. This is when you do life with people. Every relationship is different. Maybe you'll see someone once a year at a family reunion, or maybe you'll see them every day at work. Either way, the experiences you share will lay more bricks for the bridge. Of course, you may never complete the bridge. Maybe your bridge building stops after one meeting. Or maybe it's a lifetime of bricks that ends with death (yes, morbid, but also reality—we are all going to die). Don't compare your bridge building with that of others. God has gifted us in different ways.

First Corinthians 12:4-7 says, "There are different kinds of gifts, but the same Spirit distributes them. There are different kinds of service, but the same Lord. There are different kinds of working, but in all of them and in everyone it is the same God at work. Now to each one the manifestation of the Spirit is given for the common good." The common good in the Christian sense is eternity with our Creator, with our Father in heaven. Use the gifts you have, and let everyone else use the gifts they have. Gifted differently yet united with a common purpose, we all aim to grow our heavenly family.

RESOLVING CONFLICT

Despite our best efforts, we're likely to face conflict in some of our encounters. While I'll address this in greater depth in chapter 12, it's important that we be aware of this throughout the upcoming chapters because Christians should be known for their conflict-resolution skills. This doesn't mean that we compromise truth for the sake of peace, but it does mean that we shouldn't go out of our way to insert ourselves into the drama. You may be thinking to yourself, *Well, I don't insert myself into the drama, so I'm good.* Consider your social media habits. Do you dip your toes into the community page drama from time to time? I'm not talking about constructive comments that propel conversations toward resolution. I'm talking about egging people on, encouraging their ill will toward others.

There was a community my family was a part of where people got upset about a decision the school board was making. Although many community members attended the town hall meetings, most of the dirty work was done online. Cruel words were said about teachers, administrators, and parents alike. Unfortunately, some (many) of those comments were made by Christians, and that left a bad taste in the mouths of the watchers, some of whom came to me personally and said they were uncomfortable with the behavior of Christians online, especially seemingly seeking out drama and adding fuel to the fire (contrary to what Proverbs 26:20 encourages us to do). In fact, at least one person told me she no longer felt safe attending church in our community because of what she read online.

This should be difficult for you to read not because you may have participated in such ugliness, but because it's an indication that things are not right. And they aren't. They won't be until Jesus returns. In the meantime, though, we can work toward a solution. Romans 12:2 says, "Do not conform to the pattern of this world, but be transformed by the renewing of your mind. Then you will be able to test and approve what God's will is—his good, pleasing and perfect will." The world loves conflict—we even seem to revel in it if social media is to be believed. Christ followers need to be set apart.

Despite what we may see online, the good news is that it seems like we're doing a better job at conflict resolution and unity outside the church than we are within it. A 2022 Barna poll suggests, "About three in five Christians (61%) report experiencing unity most often in their homes, while 48 percent say they experience this in their friendships." The bad news is that "just over one in three (35%) says unity is found in their church."[11] This is especially disappointing because Jesus talked about unity and conflict to His followers.

In other words, He knew it would be (and would continue to be) a problem.

For example, in Matthew 18, Jesus talked about how to handle sin within the church. David Platt, in his commentary on Matthew, says that the key actions are protection, love, and restoration, which ultimately lead to forgiveness.[12] Platt suggests that a large number of church-wide conflicts would cease to exist if we would only follow step one in Jesus' plan: private correction (verse 15). "This kind of interaction," writes Platt, "is supposed to happen all the time in the context of our relationships with one another. If we would only get this first step right, we might find that about 95 percent of the work of church discipline and restoration has been taken care of before anyone else becomes involved."[13]

Craig Blomberg, in his commentary on Matthew, suggests that "there are times, of course, when it is both appropriate and necessary to correct believers for sins affecting third parties, but this can easily turn into meddling."[14] Blomberg continues: "How often personal confrontation is the last stage rather than the first in Christian complaints! It frequently seems as if the whole world knows of someone's grievances against us before we are personally approached."[15] And the Bible has some words to say about meddling and interfering in matters that aren't our business:

- "Like one who grabs a stray dog by the ears is someone who rushes into a quarrel not their own" (Proverbs 26:17).

- "Besides, they get into the habit of being idle and going about from house to house. And not only do they become idlers, but also busybodies who talk nonsense, saying things they ought not to" (1 Timothy 5:13).

- "A gossip betrays a confidence; so avoid anyone who talks too much" (Proverbs 20:19).

- "You must also rid yourselves of all such things as these: anger, rage, malice, slander, and filthy language from your lips" (Colossians 3:8).

As bridge builders, we should be especially mindful of the way we interact with everyone, inside and outside the church. Although Jesus was specifically talking about believers with other believers in Matthew 18, He also talked about unity and conflict among others. For example, look at the Beatitudes in Matthew 5:

- "Blessed are the poor in spirit" (verse 3).
- "Blessed are the meek" (verse 5).
- "Blessed are the merciful" (verse 7).
- "Blessed are the peacemakers" (verse 9).

As Blomberg explains, "All of these characteristics which Jesus labels as blessed are usually not welcomed in the world at large."[16] Yet as the Barna poll indicates, those characteristics don't seem to be welcomed in the church, either. As Christian bridge builders, we must do better at conflict resolution, both in our own homes and in the house of the Lord. Psychologist Jim Taylor suggests these simple ways to avoid conflict and increase harmony:

1. having an open mind,
2. listening well,
3. showing empathy,
4. being objective rather than emotional, and
5. seeking to understand.[17]

These suggestions align with how Jesus dealt with conflict, whether among His followers or with His adversaries. If we can achieve these in our conversations with others, we are well on our way to creating better and deeper relationships. This is important because relationships are the core of what we do as bridge builders. We'll talk more about some of these specific suggestions in Part 2.

BUILDING THE BRIDGE

The rest of this book will help you boldly and confidently share your faith while loving others the way Jesus did. Jesus calls us to be salt and light for a reason—to help point people to Him. As we engage, we are called to love one another. The Holy Spirit draws people unto Himself. That's why this book starts with a chapter about prayer and ends with a chapter about the Holy Spirit (see chapter 15).

We can serve as a bridge without exploiting others. You're not looking to score points in theological debates, but to share your faith in ways that make Christianity look attractive. The desire needs to stem from your desire to be like Jesus (see chapter 5). Jesus loved God and He loved people. And He calls His believers to love God and love others. With that in mind, let's start with the greatest bridge there is—Jesus. As John 1:1 says, "In the beginning was the Word, and the Word was with God, and the Word was God."

QUESTIONS FOR REFLECTION AND DISCUSSION

1. Have you ever made a bad first impression? How did you overcome it?

2. What does your Bible time look like? What is one step you can take now to improve it?

3. What has been the most surprising way you've created relationships with others?

4. In your experience, what has been the best way to resolve conflict?

5. What is your most pressing question about truth and apologetics?

RECOMMENDED RESOURCES

J.P. Moreland, *Love Your God with All Your Mind* (Colorado Springs, CO: NavPress, 2012)

Christopher Wright, *The Mission of God's People* (Grand Rapids, MI: Zondervan, 2010)

Lee Strobel, *The Case for Christ* (Grand Rapids, MI: Zondervan, 2016)

Andrew Newberg and Mark Robert Waldman, *Words Can Change Your Brain* (New York: Penguin Random House, 2012)

Chris Voss with Tahl Raz, *Never Split the Difference* (New York: Penguin Random House, 2016)

JESUS, THE ULTIMATE BRIDGE BUILDER

*In the first place, you can be so absolutely honest and
so absolutely wrong at the same time that I think it is
better to be a combination of cautious and polite.*

FLANNERY O'CONNOR

Have you ever seen the image where a cross is a bridge filling the gap of a giant chasm between people and God? This illustrates that Jesus is the bridge between us and His Father. Paul said this of Jesus in 1 Timothy 2:5-6: "There is one God and one mediator between God and mankind, the man Christ Jesus, who gave himself as a ransom for all people. This has now been witnessed to at the proper time." Mediator. Ransom. *For all.*

It is no small thing that Jesus, the only Son of God the Father, lived, died, rose again, and ascended to heaven. That's the hope within us. It is a big deal, and we should never be ashamed to share the good news far and wide. But aside from being the Savior of the world, Jesus gives us the best example of how to live, how to do life as a Christian, how to be a child of God. Of course, while His example is awesome, it is extraordinary and unattainable for us mere humans. We're not God. Don't forget that Jesus was fully human and fully God. But we don't get a free pass not to try to follow in Jesus' footsteps. We just need to remember that His are really big shoes to fill, and we won't be able to do it. The good news is that He's done the work only He can do so that we can carry out the part of the task that He's called us to do.

LESSONS FOR BUILDING BRIDGES

Lesson #1: Love God

> "Teacher, which is the greatest commandment in the Law?" Jesus replied: "Love the Lord your God with all your heart and with all your soul and with all your mind" (Matthew 22:36-37).

When I teach discipleship to parents, I'm often asked for practical tips to help kids understand and follow Scripture. I typically begin with the *Shema* (Hebrew for "hear"). While Jesus was speaking with some Jewish experts, they asked Him an important question about the greatest law. He didn't mince words: "Love the Lord your God with all your heart and with all your soul and with all your mind" (Matthew 22:37). In other words, love the Lord with your entire self. His response should not have been surprising to the crowd because His words echo the Shema:

> Hear, O Israel: The LORD our God, the LORD is one. *Love the LORD your God with all your heart and with all your soul and with all your strength.* These commandments that I give you today are to be on your hearts. Impress them on your children. Talk about them when you sit at home and when you walk along the road, when you lie down and when you get up. Tie them as symbols on your hands and bind them on your foreheads. Write them on the doorframes of your houses and on your gates (Deuteronomy 6:4-9, emphasis mine).

Jesus consistently and firmly impressed on His followers that they should love God with all that they had—from their brains to their toes. If we love God with our entire being, it is difficult to succumb to letting other things take priority over God. Instead, we filter everything we do through the lens of our love of God. We're less likely to fall prey to idolatry. We're more likely to stay dependent on Him. We're more likely to see people the way Jesus saw them—as image bearers of His Father. As ones He wanted to call His own.

What we prioritize sends a message to those around us. Have you ever considered that you can know what a person loves by looking at their bank statements? This can be applied to your time too. Loving God sometimes involves making tough choices about what we prioritize.

In the West, one of the more widespread examples of misplaced priorities is probably sports. Now let me be clear from the outset that I do not view sports as the enemy. My kids participate in sports, and I was an athlete long, long, long ago. I know there are benefits galore when children and adults participate in activities like team sports, including improved mental and physical health, and long-term educational and career outcomes.[1] Sports also present opportunities to live out our Christian faith—from showing good sportsmanship to exhibiting perseverance, courage, and strength on the field or court.[2]

Despite the benefits, there's no denying that sports can become an idol for some Christians. In my time on a church staff, I've seen what happens when certain sports are in season—families begin to choose practice over the pulpit. Games over gathering with other children of God. Again, I want to emphasize that sports aren't necessarily bad, but do a quick check-in on your own family. Have you placed sports (or anything else) above God? What message is this sending to others about your priorities? What idols do you need to remove from your home? Sports, social media, television, or anything else that gets in the way of prioritizing your Creator has the potential to become an idol. Don't let it happen, and if it has, be willing to make a change.

Loving God is a foundational issue for Christians. Our Creator is "a consuming fire, a jealous God" (Deuteronomy 4:24). We should place God at the top of our to-do list. Without a deep and pure and complete love for our Creator, we lack the capacity to be effective bridge builders. Our foundation will be built on sinking sand. The bedrock of loving God with all of our being helps us with the second greatest commandment: loving others.

Lesson #2: Love People

> The second [greatest commandment] is like it: "Love your neighbor as yourself" (Matthew 22:39).

One of Jesus' primary purposes was to usher in the kingdom of God. His message was radical because first-century Jewish people were expecting a war that would defeat their Roman enemies and usher in God's kingdom. Instead, Jesus spoke a message of love. How could He be the Messiah if He brought a message of shalom (wholeness and peace)? He was transforming preconceived notions about what it meant to be the people of God.

Theologian N.T. Wright explains that there were four parts to Jesus' mission: "invitation, welcome, challenge, and summons."[3] Jesus opened with the gospel (a message of hope grounded in His role as the Savior), and then He "offered to all and sundry a welcome that… shocked many of his contemporaries to the core…He was welcoming sinners into fellowship with himself *precisely as part of his kingdom announcement*."[4] His fellowship was rooted in love, for His Father and for us. With love, we see a transformation.

Christ-followers are challenged to change their thinking and their way of life. Ultimately, we are called to love just as our Savior showed us. Time and time again, Jesus called His followers to a life of love.

For example, let's look at Jesus' interaction with Zacchaeus (see Luke 19:1-9). You know the guy—the short man who climbed a tree to get a glimpse of Jesus. It is at this point that I'd queue the music in children's church.[5]

Before we continue discussing Zacchaeus, let's talk about tax collectors in the first century. Keep in mind that they were not peoples' favorite to be around. They were typically Jewish men who worked for the Romans, and they were considered traitors by other Jews. Tax collectors were often wealthy because they took their wages from the money they collected, and they oftentimes overcharged so they could take a big cut for themselves. It is not surprising, then, that they were hated and distrusted by their own people.

Jesus once told a parable about a Pharisee (Jewish leaders known for two things: their strict keeping of the law and their pride) and a tax collector (Luke 18:9-14). Jesus said both men went to the temple to pray. The Pharisee used his prayer time to brag about how great he was compared to so many others, including the nearby tax collector. The Pharisee also boasted about his spiritual practices like fasting and tithing. The tax collector, on the other hand, simply asked God for mercy.

Jesus used this parable to show that the one asking for mercy was justified by God. It didn't matter what his reputation was or what his spiritual life looked like. Jesus saw him as a child of God, one who admitted he was a sinner and in need of the Lord's mercy. By using a tax collector in His parable, Jesus was showing His cards to those gathered around Him—someone's past doesn't define their future, and their future shouldn't be underestimated when the power of God is involved. All are worthy of love, forgiveness, and shalom.

With that in mind, let's get back to Zacchaeus. He wasn't just any old tax collector, he was the *chief* tax collector, a title that probably means he was in charge of a tax district—all the more reason for him to be hated. He was so desperate to see Jesus that he climbed a tree to get a glimpse of the Messiah, and Jesus took the time to meet him: "Zacchaeus, come down immediately. I must stay at your house today" (Luke 19:5). Jesus wasn't dumb. He knew people would immediately pass judgment. How could He possibly deign to dine with a sinner like a tax collector?

Jesus saw Zacchaeus and loved him. He gave Zacchaeus an opportunity to welcome Him into his home, and then Jesus welcomed Zacchaeus into God's kingdom. We don't know exactly what this scene looked like, but I imagine a warm embrace was involved (hugs were not uncommon for the first-century Jews). How the crowd must have reacted to that!

New Testament scholar Darrell Bock writes that "if Jesus had used the crowd's standard of association, he would never have addressed Zacchaeus."[6] Instead, Jesus defied tradition and reached out to Zacchaeus and offered him salvation. Zacchaeus more than accepted Jesus' offer—he changed his life. Zacchaeus's transformation led him to give half of what he owned to the poor and return the money he had stolen from people fourfold. Bock explains that "such faith is not an intellectual exercise; it is a change of worldview."[7]

Jesus builds bridges to us, God's image bearers (His creation), because He loves us. He's the bridge because He would do anything to keep us safe from harm. He offers salvation to all who will come to Him. Jesus welcomes us with open arms, and as His disciples, we should do the same to others.

Love is transformative. The first time I held our daughters after they were born, I knew I'd never be the same. I'd do anything to protect them and to save them from harm. Jesus does this better than anyone. He sets the standard of how to love others well. When Zacchaeus was approached by Jesus, he was approached by Love Himself. We're talking about the Savior of the world, the One who would leave the 99 to save the one (Matthew 18:12).

In Zacchaeus's case, Jesus left the crowd to be with the man in the tree. Showing genuine love for others means being willing to step away from the crowd and reach out to the one on the sideline, even if that one is shunned by the community. Love well, because love builds bridges better than anything else.

Lesson #3: Be Gentle

> Take my yoke upon you and learn from me, for I am gentle and humble in heart, and you will find rest for your souls (Matthew 11:29).

> Let your gentleness be evident to all. The Lord is near (Philippians 4:5).

Gentleness is a key factor in building bridges because people don't want to be confronted with rudeness or disrespect. After all, "a gentle answer turns away wrath, but a harsh word stirs up anger" (Proverbs 15:1). Put another way, do what Jesus taught: "Do to others what you would have them do to you" (Matthew 7:12). In His Sermon on the Mount, Jesus said, "Blessed are the meek [gentle], for they will inherit the earth" (Matthew 5:5). Jesus also described Himself as "gentle and humble in heart" (Matthew 11:29). Ultimately, gentleness was a big deal to our Savior, and it should be a big deal to us too.

Jesus regularly showed gentleness in His interactions with the least of these (people like you and me). For example, in Matthew 8, when a leper approached Jesus, instead of shooing him away as others most assuredly did, our Lord reached out, touched him, and healed him. In our day and age, it might be difficult to imagine why this was such an extraordinary reaction. Lepers were shunned by others. They were outcasts. They were probably like the Factionless in the Divergent series. I'm still a little disappointed with how the series ended, but author Veronica Roth expertly showed us what it may have looked like to be a leper in Jesus' time. Lepers, like the

Factionless, were left to suffer and die alone, often due to circumstances beyond their control.

There was no cure for leprosy, and because lepers were "unclean," they couldn't have contact with anyone who didn't have the disease. And yet, like the Abnegation faction in *Divergent*, Jesus showed lepers gentleness and mercy. We see Jesus interact with more lepers in Luke 17, and once again, He shows them gentleness rather than pushing them away (though they kept their distance on their own).[8] What was considered extraordinary seems to have been a normal thing for our Savior.

Another example of Jesus' gentleness is His interaction with children in Matthew 19. Some adults brought children to Jesus, but His disciples rebuked them.[9] These children were likely infants, and the disciples probably assumed that Jesus wouldn't want to interact with babies, especially since He had been discussing a very adult topic, eunuchs, shortly before (verse 12). Apparently, nothing could have been further from the truth because "Jesus said, 'Let the little children come to me, and do not hinder them, for the kingdom of heaven belongs to such as these'" (verse 14). He then laid His hands on the babies and blessed them.

Finally (though there are many examples of Jesus' gentleness sprinkled throughout the Gospels), consider Jesus' exchange with the widow in Luke 7. Her dead son was being carried out of the city gates. Jesus went up to her and comforted her, telling her not to cry (verse 13). As a mom, I can only imagine the depths of despair the woman was feeling, especially knowing she'd already lost her husband and had now lost her only son. After consoling the widow, Jesus raised the child from the dead and "gave him back to his mother" (verse 15). The beauty of this example is that Jesus first extended support to the woman *and then* healed her son. It is no wonder that Jesus left us with the Holy Spirit after He ascended to heaven. He knew that humanity needs a comforter because "in this world [there will be] trouble" (John 16:33). The good news—the hope—is that Jesus has "overcome the world."

Keep in mind that gentleness is one of the fruits of the Spirit (Galatians 5:23). It is a hallmark of Jesus' character, and we have easy access to the gift of gentleness from the Holy Spirit. May our gentleness show people Jesus.

Lesson #4: Bring People Together

> Where two or three gather in my name, there am I with them (Matthew 18:20).

> One day as Jesus was standing by the Lake of Gennesaret, the people were crowding around him and listening to the word of God (Luke 5:1).

I have a task for you. The next time you're at the store, pick 12 people at random and tell them to leave everything behind and follow you. See what they say. If they go along with your ruse, how long do you think it will be before there is conflict among them? How long until someone attempts to usurp your authority? How long before someone leaves feeling betrayed? My guess is that this wouldn't work out very well for you. It is *possible* there would be a few in the group who would get along to achieve a common goal, but because of differences in culture, religion, background, political affiliation, and all the other things that make us unique, it would be difficult to make it happen with all 12.

And yet, this worked for Jesus. I know, He's God and we're human. But He was human too. He was not well known when He called the Twelve. He was a God-man on a mission to save the universe from destruction, and He knew just the men who would help Him complete that mission. But when we look at the makeup of the Twelve, it seems difficult to reconcile the situation—how did it work? *Jesus.*

He is how it worked. He brought people together, and their lives were changed forever. You're not Jesus (I know I say that a lot, but it's true). You're His disciple. And He told His followers to make disciples (Matthew 28:19-20).

You may be thinking that it didn't work because Judas was a part of the Twelve. Why would Jesus include someone like Judas, someone He knew would betray Him? Some New Testament scholars think that Jesus was deliberate in His decision because He needed Judas to betray Him so that prophecy could be fulfilled. Other scholars say Judas is a perfect illustration of humanity's free will—he literally knew Jesus and yet he rejected Him. The reality is that Jesus, as fully God and fully human, knew what the end result would be of His decision to call Judas to become one of the Twelve. Despite His foreknowledge, Jesus reached out with love to Judas. His refrain while on the cross, "Father, forgive them, for they do not know what they are doing," could have also applied to Judas.

As a bridge builder, you will likely get hurt. You may even be betrayed by someone you trust. Stand firm in truth, knowing that ultimately, each human being must decide for themselves whether they will follow our King. Pray for others as Jesus prayed for those who killed Him.

Jesus brought people together, and it worked. He made fishermen fishers of men. You might look at your Christian friends and think to yourself, "How does this even work? How can we all be Christ followers and yet be so different?" It is because Jesus is still bringing people together by calling them to Himself. What's so incredibly special is that we get to be bridge builders right alongside Him.

Lesson #5: Offer Hope

> Jesus answered, "Everyone who drinks this water will
> be thirsty again, but whoever drinks the water I give

them will never thirst. Indeed, the water I give them will become in them a spring of water welling up to eternal life" (John 4:13-14).

Shortly before writing this, I got back from camp with 28 kids from my church. While we were there, we learned about how heavy life in the world can be (remember how Jesus said there would be trouble?). The heaviness is because of the fallenness of creation. The pastor at the camp used brownie mix to illustrate how sin ruins things. He made the mix according to the instructions. Then he proceeded to add rocks and dirt and leaves to it. That which was good was then destroyed. That's humanity in a nutshell. That is why the Father sent us Jesus, who is the hope within us. Jesus shared this hope with the many people He met while He was here on earth.

For example, let's look at Jesus' conversation with the woman at the well in John 4. This woman was living with a man who was not her husband, and she was being shunned. She visited the well at a time when no one else would be there. In this instance, though, Jesus was there, and He was thirsty. He asked her for some water, which probably blew her mind because she was a Samaritan and He was a Jew (the two people groups had a long-standing conflict that we'll address more in chapter 11). In response to her confusion, Jesus told her about "living water" (verse 10). This was the first time in John that Jesus revealed Himself as the Messiah. He told the woman about eternal life and said, "I am he," the Messiah. He offered her hope, and she was so thrilled about it that she went and told everyone about Him.

Jesus did this again as He was breathing His final breaths (see Luke 23). One of the criminals being crucified beside Jesus mocked Him. But the other admitted his sin and acknowledged that Jesus was the Messiah. He asked Jesus to remember him. Instead of focusing on His own pain and circumstances, Jesus offered the man hope. He said, "Truly I tell you, today you will be with me in paradise" (verse 43). I imagine that at that moment, the man felt enormous hope and peace and joy, knowing that his freedom was just around the corner.

The world needs hope, and as bridge builders, we can give it to them. We can show the world that despite our sin and wretchedness, we are redeemed in Christ. We will be reconciled with the Father, not because of anything we can do but because of what Christ has done for us.

Lesson #6: Make Disciples

> Jesus came to them and said, "All authority in heaven and on earth has been given to me. Therefore go and make disciples of all nations, baptizing them in the name of the Father and of the Son and of the Holy Spirit, and teaching them to obey everything I have commanded you. And surely I am with you always, to the very end of the age" (Matthew 28:18-20).

One of my favorite miracles of Jesus is that of the boats overflowing with fish. If you recall the narrative in Luke 5, Jesus is teaching a group of people at the edge of the Sea of Galilee. He uses Simon Peter's boat as a stage so that the people can hear Him better. Then He turns to Simon Peter and says, "Put out into deep water, and let down the nets for a catch" (verse 4). Picture it. Simon Peter and his buddies had been out at sea all night, and they hadn't caught a thing. Then this teacher they don't know has the audacity to tell them to put out the nets. As if things had changed. They had, of course, yet they didn't know that. But something within Simon Peter was moved, and he obeyed Jesus, despite his skepticism. Then, the fish came, and the nets were filled.

Simon Peter eventually repents, and Jesus calls him to be His disciple. The interaction shows us that Jesus met Simon Peter where he was, both physically and spiritually. Simon was sinful, tired, hungry, and disheartened. And Jesus gave Simon Peter what he needed: forgiveness, peace, and a whole lot of fish. Jesus' willingness to reveal His power and deity led to Simon Peter's willingness to serve Jesus. What a beautiful example of making disciples. Was Simon Peter perfect? No. Was he willing? Yes, and Jesus knew what was to come.

The rest of Simon Peter's story is found in the first half of Acts, directly following Jesus' Great Commission in Matthew 28. Simon Peter carries out the mission—he leads the early church (Matthew 16:18). He was the bridge between Jesus' ministry and Paul's. William Steuart McBirnie describes Peter's role like this:

> The book of Acts was originally written to show the transition of Christianity from a Jewish sect to a world faith. Therefore, the story of Peter is told there so that we might see how Peter, who had the leadership position in the early church, carried the gospel beyond the boundaries of the Jewish world into the Gentile world. Then the story is transferred to Paul who became uniquely the apostle to the Gentiles.[10]

The result of Jesus' investment in Simon Peter was the transformation of Simon Peter's life and the expansion of God's kingdom. Peter became a bridge builder. Before Jesus ascended to heaven, He said, "Go and make disciples of all nations, baptizing them in the name of the Father and of the Son and of the Holy Spirit, and teaching them to obey everything I have commanded you" (Matthew 28:19-20). As Jesus' disciples, we have the responsibility (mandated by Christ Himself) to evangelize. Such work can be daunting and could result in trials and tribulations as it did for the original disciples. And yet the result is furthering God's kingdom. Building bridges is kingdom work. Go. Make disciples. Baptize. Teach.

BUILDING THE BRIDGE

The number one bridge builder in the Bible is Jesus. The six lessons we covered in this chapter were:

- Love God.
- Love people.
- Be gentle.
- Bring people together.
- Offer hope.
- Make disciples.

Jesus illustrated these frequently throughout His ministry on earth, and as Christ followers, we should make every effort to follow His lead. Being a bridge builder means striving "to act justly and to love mercy and to walk humbly with your God" (Micah 6:8). By applying these lessons in our own lives, not only will we transform our world, but we will also further the kingdom of God.

QUESTIONS FOR REFLECTION AND DISCUSSION

1. What two or three lessons from Jesus can you apply in your own life when working to build bridges with others?

2. In what ways do you already try to walk like Jesus and build bridges the way He did?

3. Which interaction involving Jesus resonated the most with you?

4. Think of someone who needs hope. Pray for them and be like Jesus—let them know how they can have freedom from their sin through our Savior's sacrifice.

5. What does it mean to be a disciple? What does it mean to *make* disciples (see Matthew 28:19-20)?

RECOMMENDED RESOURCES

The Gospels of Matthew, Mark, Luke, and John

Rebecca McLaughlin, *Confronting Jesus* (Wheaton, IL: Crossway, 2022)[11]

William Steuart McBirnie, *The Search for the Twelve Apostles* (Carol Stream, IL: Tyndale, 1974)

Mark A. Noll, *Jesus Christ and the Life of the Mind* (Grand Rapids, MI: Eerdmans, 2013)

Norman L. Geisler and Patrick Zukeran, *The Apologetics of Jesus: A Caring Approach to Dealing with Doubters* (Ada, MI: Baker, 2009)

PAUL, THE GOSPEL-CENTRIC BRIDGE BUILDER

Let us therefore make every effort to do what
leads to peace and to mutual edification.

ROMANS 14:19

As I was putting together ideas for this book, I knew it had to have a chapter about Paul, but I was uncertain about doing that, for a few reasons. First, I was concerned because so many Christians are already familiar with Paul and his teachings, and therefore, they might skip this chapter, and I wanted the chapter to be read. Second, I was worried that people might think I was elevating Paul to Jesus' level, which is not the case—Jesus is our Savior, not Paul. Finally, there are some who believe that Paul's teachings contradicted what Jesus taught, such that the differences between Paul and Jesus should make us second-guess using Paul too often as an example.

As to the first issue, this chapter may reinforce what you've already learned about Paul, but I hope to also offer lessons specific to bridge building that you may not have already considered. As to the second issue, Jesus will always be the main person in Christianity, not Paul. Paul himself boldly proclaimed that without Christ and the resurrection, "our preaching is useless and so is your faith" (1 Corinthians 15:14). Jesus should be the foundation of our faith, just as He was the foundation of Paul's faith. And there is a thing or two or twelve we can learn from the apostle. Finally, I'd like to dig a little deeper into the third concern because if Paul contradicted Jesus, we've got bigger fish to fry in this chapter than simply addressing how Paul built bridges with people.

From the outset, I can assure you that Paul's teachings don't contradict anything Jesus ever said.

New Testament scholar N.T. Wright illustrates the relationship between Jesus' and Paul's teachings by saying that Jesus is like a composer, and Paul is like the person teaching people how to sing what Jesus has composed. Another New Testament scholar, Craig Blomberg, explains that there are certainly distinctions between both men's teachings, but that can be explained in part by the fact that they had different audiences and different purposes. Jesus was revealing Himself to others, while Paul was pointing others to Jesus.[1]

Ultimately, Jesus laid the framework for Christianity, and Paul helped usher in the religion, pointing to Jesus and redemption throughout his ministry. Paul was the bearer of good news, not the author of it. Despite some differences, upon reflection, we can see a bridge between what Jesus taught and what Paul taught, and it is an effective bridge with a strong structure and foundation. It is because of Paul's constructive evangelism that I've included a chapter about him, and my hope is that you'll learn a little more about Paul and acquire some lessons from him for your bridge-building Rolodex.[2]

SAUL'S TRANSFORMATION

I'm starting with Paul's life and conversion just in case you haven't heard the account or you need a reminder. Paul's history is a vital part of understanding why he is such a formative force in the Bible. We first learn about Paul when he was primarily known by another name, Saul (though he was still sometimes called Saul following his conversion), and his first appearance in Scripture almost seems like an afterthought. The book of Acts describes the years following Jesus' ascension into heaven, during which the disciples are setting up the early church, and Christ followers are already facing persecution.

Acts 6–7 hones in on Stephen, one of seven people selected by the disciples to serve food to the growing congregation of Hellenistic Jews who had become Christians (Acts 6:1). Stephen was making waves (as the disciples often did) for performing great wonders and miracles. He was eventually put on trial by Jewish leaders and was sentenced to death. This is when we meet Saul, at Stephen's stoning: "Meanwhile, the witnesses laid their clothes at the feet of a young man named Saul" (Acts 7:58). As Stephen was about to be stoned, Saul was present and "in hearty agreement with putting him to death" (Acts 8:1 NASB 1995).

We don't hear about Saul again until Acts 9. Saul is still hating Christians, and he's still pushing for their deaths. In fact, in Acts 9, we find him rounding up followers of "the Way" to bring them to Jerusalem for persecution (verse 1-2). Then Jesus shows up. After being struck blind, Saul continues onward to Damascus and is (reluctantly) visited by a disciple named Ananias, who tells him "Brother Saul, the Lord—Jesus, who appeared to you on the road as you were coming here—has sent me so that you may see again and be filled with the Holy Spirit" (verse 17).

Saul was baptized and went on to become arguably the best bridge builder in Scripture besides Jesus because his course changed so dramatically when he was indwelled by the Holy Spirit and realized the hope of the gospel. That's why Saul, or Paul, gets a whole chapter in this book—because there is much to learn from his story.

LEARNING FROM PAUL'S EXAMPLE

Lesson #1: Let God Change You and Use You

> I want you to know, brothers and sisters, that the gospel I preached is not of human origin. I did not receive it

from any man, nor was I taught it; rather, I received it by
revelation from Jesus Christ (Galatians 1:11-12).

What is so striking about the early church leaders is the fact that
many of them experienced such major changes in their lives upon following Jesus. The ten-dollar word for this is *sanctification*, which, put
simply, is to be set apart for God's special purposes. They were indwelled
by the Holy Spirit. And the changes were palpable and obvious. Paul's
transformation was clear—he went from being someone who sought
out the persecution and death of Christ followers to someone who
wanted to spread the gospel to everyone. He was uniquely gifted for
such a role in the early church. He was "set apart" (Romans 1:1).[3]

Paul knew Hebrew Scripture well. As a Roman citizen and Phar-
isaic Jewish boy raised in the early first century, he probably learned
to read by studying the Hebrew Bible. He also likely had to memorize and recite large portions of Scripture. Luke wrote in Acts 22:3
that Paul was "thoroughly trained in the law" by Gamaliel, a person of high authority in the Great Sanhedrin in Jerusalem. Paul was
probably fluent in both Greek and Hebrew. He was "advancing in
Judaism beyond many of [his] own age" and "was extremely zealous"
(Galatians 1:14).

In addition to knowing Scripture, Paul was well versed in culture.
Paul grew up in Tarsus, a place of great learning. It was also a pros-
perous seaport city on the Mediterranean. Young men would travel
to Tarsus to learn "philosophy, rhetoric, law, mathematics, astronomy,
medicine, geography, and botany."[4] It should be of no surprise that
Paul had access to university-level content from a young age, and it
seems, based on his letters and from the way Luke describes him in
Acts, that Paul was highly educated and culturally attuned—so much
so that he could relate well to various audiences.

All that to say, the lesson here is not that you need to be highly
educated. Rather, you want to let God change you and use you based

on the unique gifts and experiences He's given to you. Remember, Paul wrote in 1 Corinthians 12 that "there are different kinds of gifts, but the same Spirit distributes them. There are different kinds of service, but the same Lord. There are different kinds of working, but in all of them and in everyone it is the same God at work. Now to each one the manifestation of the Spirit is given for the common good" (verses 4-7). Let the Spirit indwell you and use you for His purposes with whichever gifts He has bestowed upon you.

Lesson #2: Be a Willing Vessel

> In a large house there are articles not only of gold and silver, but also of wood and clay; some are for special purposes and some for common use. Those who cleanse themselves from the latter will be instruments for special purposes, made holy, useful to the Master and prepared to do any good work (2 Timothy 2:20-21).

Have you ever tried to excuse yourself from something because you didn't feel qualified? Maybe you don't volunteer with your church's children's ministry because you're "not good with kids," or you don't go out and serve the homeless because "there are others who are more gifted in that area." You may remember how Moses tried to tell God that He was wrong in calling Moses to lead the Israelites out of Egypt. Moses was afraid he wasn't well-spoken enough or well-enough equipped to do what God was telling him to do.

Exodus 3:11 explains, "Moses said to God, 'Who am I, that I should go to Pharaoh and bring the Israelites out of Egypt?'" But God didn't falter with His command—"And God said, 'I will be with you. And this will be the sign to you that it is I who have sent you: When you have brought the people out of Egypt, you will worship God on this mountain'" (verse 12). Moses wasn't exactly a willing vessel, but God still used him. How much better, though, when someone is willing? That's what we see with Paul.

I mentioned earlier that Ananias was reluctant to visit Paul prior to his transformation because of Paul's reputation for violence and hostility. God, however, had plans and said, "Go! This man is my *chosen instrument* to proclaim my name" (Acts 9:15, emphasis added). Not only was Paul a *chosen* instrument, but he was a *willing* instrument. He considered it an honor to be used by God: "We have this treasure in jars of clay to show that this all-surpassing power is from God and not from us. We are hard pressed on every side, but not crushed; perplexed, but not in despair; persecuted, but not abandoned; struck down, but not destroyed" (2 Corinthians 4:7-9). Paul consistently encouraged others to be willing vessels for the Lord (2 Timothy 2:20-21). So, even if you feel underqualified or you think someone else might be better at bridge building than you are, if God is calling you to do His work, He will give you what you need, so long as you are willing.

Lesson #3: Be Humble and Sacrificial

> I know what it is to be in need, and I know what it is to have plenty. I have learned the secret of being content in any and every situation, whether well fed or hungry, whether living in plenty or in want. I can do all this through him who gives me strength (Philippians 4:12-13).

Have you ever heard the metaphor "thorn in the flesh" or "thorn in the side"? The phrase originates from the Old Testament, in Numbers 33:55. God told Moses to drive out the pagan inhabitants from Canaan, or they would become "thorns in [their] sides." Paul used the phrase in 2 Corinthians 12:7 and called his thorn "a messenger of Satan." He had just finished boasting about his suffering, which included a litany of awful experiences, such as hunger, floggings, sleeplessness, and shipwrecks (2 Corinthians 11:21-30).[5] He had also endured opposition and rejection. Talk about thorns! What Paul endured is a far cry from what I sometimes consider thorns in my flesh, like long drop-off lines at school or my grocery store forgetting a few items in my curbside order or the musicians playing too loudly at church.

Minor annoyances should not be elevated to thorn status. Paul suffered agony for the gospel; he wore his thorns as though they were badges because they showed his weakness and emphasized his need of a Savior. His thorns helped keep him humble. He was forced to rely on God. So, when you stumble upon a thorn while bridge building and sharing your faith, whether it is argument or outright rejection, wear that thorn like it is your favorite flower, recognizing that "[you] are to God the pleasing aroma of Christ among those who are being saved and those who are perishing" (2 Corinthians 2:15).

Lesson #4: Offer Truth with Love

> Speaking the truth in love, we will grow to become in every respect the mature body of him who is the head, that is, Christ (Ephesians 4:15).

Christians are facing a crisis: How can we truly love people and tell them the truth at the same time? Truth has become relative. In a culture where *my* truth is *the* truth even if it conflicts with *your* truth, it is now considered unloving to point out errors in someone's worldview.[6] But, as preacher Warren W. Wiersbe wrote, "Truth without love is brutality, and love without truth is hypocrisy."[7] Essentially, it is effectively unloving to not share the truth with others. And guess what? Non-Christians are often surprised (and not always in a bad way) by our willingness to share our faith.

In 2010, magician Penn Jillette shared that a man approached him after a show and gave him a Bible.[8] "It was really wonderful. I believe he knew that I was an atheist, but he was not defensive. And he looked me right in the eyes. And he was truly complimentary... It didn't seem like empty flattery. He was really kind and nice and sane." He went on to give an indictment of Christians who do not share the gospel. "If you believe there's a heaven and hell," he said, "and you think, well, it's not really worth telling them this because it would make it socially awkward...How much do you have to hate somebody to not proselytize?"[9]

Jillette expressed the expectation that more Christians should share their faith openly, especially if they believe that they possess the truth and belief leads to eternal life. Otherwise, we don't love atheists—we hate them. Jillette's perspective is hopeful for Christ followers, especially in the context of this book. What especially touched Jillette about this interaction was the man's gentleness and kindness. He wasn't controlling or domineering. He was loving.

Be honest with yourself. Did you just break out into a sweat thinking about approaching an outspoken atheist and offering them a Bible? You're not alone! Doing that can be intimidating. Thankfully, though, we have a lot we can learn from Paul regarding truth telling with love.

It all starts with love. Paul spent quite a bit of time talking about love, especially in 1 Corinthians 13. If you've been to a wedding, you've likely heard the key verses quoted: "Love is patient, love is kind. It does not envy, it does not boast, it is not proud. It does not dishonor others, it is not self-seeking, it is not easily angered, it keeps no record of wrongs. Love does not delight in evil but rejoices with the truth" (verses 4-6).

Love is powerful because it speaks when words cannot. The ways you show generosity and patience and forgiveness speak love to those around you. When we love others, we're willing to take risks and be bold. We want to fully engage on a personal level with people. And we can't fathom not sharing the gospel because we know of its great importance. Truth is easy, love isn't. If you speak the truth without love, you've lost the heart of the gospel.

Lesson #5: Be Gospel Centric

> I am not ashamed of the gospel, because it is the power of God that brings salvation to everyone who believes: first to the Jew, then to the Gentile (Romans 1:16).

As I write this book, I have a small two-sided leather sign hanging on my wall—one side says, "Now is a good time to pray about that," and the other side says, "Make people your favorite." A friend made it, and I think it is perfect for anyone who is working toward building bridges with others. We've already talked at length about how vital prayer is (chapter 1). Now let's talk about people. The best way to make people your favorite is to see them as God sees them—as image bearers who need a Savior. Make people your favorite because God loves them, and you know the eternal life-giving salve that is the gospel.

After his conversion and transformation, Paul made people his favorite. Perhaps we see this best illustrated in Acts 17. Don't jump right to the narrative about the unknown god, though. Start at the beginning. You'll find that Paul had a custom of stopping at Jewish synagogues when he arrived at new places. In Acts 17, Paul spent "three Sabbath days" reasoning from the Scriptures with the leaders at the synagogue, "explaining and proving that the Messiah had to suffer and rise from the dead" (verses 2-3). He spent time persuading (Greek, *peitho*) people of the validity of the gospel message because he knew that was what they needed.

Paul was confident in his message. He had experienced real change in his own life because of Jesus, and he had a strong desire to impart that message to others so that they could be changed too. And he saw results: "Some of the Jews were persuaded and joined Paul and Silas, as did a large number of God-fearing Greeks and quite a few prominent women" (verse 4). I'm sure he was encouraged by these outcomes, but it wasn't all sunshine and rainbows. In the verses following, we learn that Paul faced opposition and eventually landed in Athens—the site of his famous speech on Mars Hill.

To understand the beauty of Paul's actions in the second half of Acts 17, you need to know a bit about Athens. This city was full of people and gods. Polytheism was king. So was philosophy. Athens was home to people like Socrates and Aristotle. This is the city Plato said was "very great and very famous for its wisdom and power." Paul knew what he was getting into, and he entered the fray with poise, even when some of those observing him called him a "babbler" (verse 18). Paul saw the idols and the opportunity for the gospel to bring those idols down.

When asked to engage at the Areopagus (Mars Hill), Paul seized the moment. He started by acknowledging the beliefs of the men in attendance as well as the altars around the city, including one "to an Unknown God" (verse 23). He even quoted a famous poet, Aratus, to speak in terms they would understand (verse 28). Then he showed his cards. He boldly and in no uncertain terms shared the gospel. This was an example of Paul's desire to become "all things to all people," as he said in 1 Corinthians 9:22. He did so because his desire and calling led him to take great risks to show the truth to others: that Jesus lived, died, and was resurrected for the forgiveness of their sins so that they could be reunited with the Father and have eternal life.

Lesson #6: Pray and Be Led by the Holy Spirit

> I pray that out of his glorious riches he may strengthen you with power through his Spirit in your inner being so that Christ may dwell in your hearts through faith (Ephesians 3:16-17).

As I said in chapter 1, Paul's life was full of prayer. He prayed often and openly. He frequently started his letters with prayer and ended them with blessings. He intervened on behalf of the lost. He thanked God. Paul also took Jesus seriously when He said He was leaving us a helpmate, the Holy Spirit. If the Spirit told him to go, he went. If the Spirit told him to stay, he stayed. Chapter 1 gives specific tips on how to incorporate prayer into your life's rhythms. Chapter 15 will remind you of your Helper, the Holy Spirit. Keep in mind that it is He who brings people unto Himself (John 6:44; 12:32). As you embark on a life of bridge building, "now is a great time to pray about that."[10]

BUILDING THE BRIDGE

Much can be learned from the apostle Paul. The six bridge-building lessons we covered in this chapter were:

- Let God change you and use you.

- Be a willing vessel.

- Be humble and sacrificial.

- Offer truth with love.

- Be gospel centric.

- Pray and be led by the Holy Spirit.

Paul's story could have ended badly—a murderous soldier who was bloodthirsty for Christ followers. Instead, he was transformed by the power of our Savior and used his gifts for good. He had a unique ability to connect with all types of people, and those people were changed because of his willingness to share his own life story and experiences with them. Sometimes, building a bridge means being vulnerable and willing to open up. By sharing our transformation stories, we open the door to share the hope within us.

QUESTIONS FOR REFLECTION AND DISCUSSION

1. What lesson from Paul is one that you already do well when building bridges with others?

2. What lesson from Paul could you improve upon as you work toward building bridges with others?

3. Can you think of a movie or book that could help you share the gospel with others?

4. In what ways can you make people your favorite in terms of sharing the gospel with them?

RECOMMENDED RESOURCES

N.T. Wright, *Paul and the Faithfulness of God* (Minneapolis, MN: Fortress Press, 2013)

"The Complete Story of Paul: The Apostles to the Gentiles," *Bible Unbound*, YouTube, https://www.youtube.com/watch?v =LTBS0NMWSPY

Craig Blomberg, *From Pentecost to Patmos* (Nashville, TN: B&H Academic, 2006) (especially chapters 2–8)

OTHER BRIDGE-BUILDING LESSONS FROM SCRIPTURE AND MODERNITY

Judging others makes us blind, whereas love is illuminating.
By judging others we blind ourselves to our own evil and to
the grace which others are just as entitled to as we are.

DIETRICH BONHOEFFER[1]

There are more lessons about bridge building to be learned from Jesus and Paul, and we can never have too many lessons when we're talking about potentially life-changing relationships and conversations. Scripture is full of examples, some of which I'll highlight in this chapter, but I'll also bring in some examples from recent history. As poet and Pulitzer Prize winner Robert Penn Warren once said, "History cannot give us a program for the future, but it can give us a fuller understanding of ourselves, and of our common humanity, so that we can better face the future."[2] Bridge building has been happening since God called people to be His messengers, and what more can we do than learn from the examples that have come before us and apply the good lessons to our own experiences?

EXAMPLES WE CAN LEARN FROM

The Priests of the Hebrew Scriptures

Lesson: Take the message to the people.

In the Old Testament, priests were to serve as a bridge between the Jewish people and Yahweh. The Latin word *pontifex*, often used to describe a priest, means "bridge builder." Deuteronomy 33 describes the responsibilities of priests, including protecting the tabernacle, performing sacrifices, and teaching people about God. They were mediators who helped reconcile God with His people long before God sent His only Son to us.

One example of a bridge-building priest was Melchizedek (try saying that fast three times in a row). We first meet him in Genesis 14, and we read about him again in Hebrews. He's the very first person given the title priest in the Hebrew Scripture. Jesus was even described as a priest in the order of Melchizedek, an order that required only one sacrifice, not endless sacrifices, like the order of the Levites (see Hebrews 7). All that to say, Melchizedek was an important bridge builder, opening the door to a relationship between God and His people, but also as the beginning of the line of priests that Jesus would ultimately join.

The New Testament says that we "are a chosen people, a royal *priesthood*, a holy nation, God's special possession, that [we] may declare the praises of him who called [us] out of darkness into his wonderful light" (1 Peter 2:9, emphasis added). Yes, you are a priest if you're a child of God as a result of accepting forgiveness through Jesus Christ. There are responsibilities that come with this title, including being a bridge builder and teaching others about God's Word. It is a title that you share with Christ Himself and one you should not take lightly. Wear it with honor, never forgetting who you represent and why.

Simon Peter

Lesson: Be a willing vessel.

You might be thinking, *Didn't we talk about being a willing vessel in the last chapter?* Yes, we did. That was one of the lessons we learned from Paul, but I'm highlighting it again with Peter. It is probably safe to say that all the disciples began their time with Jesus as willing vessels, even Judas. Though Judas lost his way, the rest of the disciples continued to be willing after Christ's death, including Simon Peter.

In chapter 3, I talked about the miracle of the fishes and Simon Peter. You may recall that Peter had faith Jesus was "the Messiah, the Son of the living God" (Matthew 16:16). Following his proclamation of Jesus' identity, Peter and the other disciples were presented opportunities to represent Christ. No pressure. Unfortunately, Peter would deny Jesus three times, despite previously acknowledging Him as the Messiah. And yet, Peter persisted in his faith, and after Jesus ascended to heaven, Peter helped lead the apostolic church.

One of Peter's first leadership jobs was to find a replacement for Judas. I imagine that Peter and the others were emotional at this point. Not only had Jesus left them for an unknown amount of time, but they were probably still reeling from Judas's betrayal of their Savior. Recently, I experienced an upheaval of sorts in my own friendship circle. One day, the friend was there, and the next day, they weren't. For those of us who experienced the sudden loss, the grief ebbed and flowed. Some days were worse than others, and yet the work still had to be done, without our friend by our side. I'm guessing this is how the apostles felt about finding Judas's replacement. The task was hard, but it was necessary, and Peter was willing to help lead them through it, and he used God's Word as guidance, pointing the apostles to Scripture—Psalms 69:25 and 109:8. Although he was most certainly feeling pain, he continued to do the work the Lord had called him to do.

Peter also worked to continue to reconcile with the Samaritans, just as Jesus had taught in so many of His parables. He healed people in Jesus' name. He went far and wide to share the good news. Peter eventually was crucified upside down for his faith, which was apparently unwavering. Did he build bridges perfectly? No. In fact, at one point, because of peer pressure, he essentially ruined the relationships Paul had built between the Jews and Gentiles in Antioch (Galatians 2). Show him some grace, though, because, as Scot McKnight notes, "Peter had lived a sheltered life…and changes that Peter's new ministry involved were difficult for him…Consistency in Christian living is not conformity and uniformity. Consistency is measured by listening to God's word, to Christ, and to the Spirit of God."[3]

To follow Jesus well doesn't mean perfection—only God is perfect. Instead, how do we adjust to change and continue to allow God to transform us to His will? We are clay; He is the potter (Jeremiah 18:1-6). Quit trying to take the reins; instead, allow Him to lead you where He wishes you to go. And keep getting back up again because God wants to use you for His purposes.

John the Baptist

Lesson: Don't be afraid to ask questions.

John and Jesus were cousins, and both had incredible beginnings, not the least of which is that both sets of parents were approached by angels before conception (see Luke 1).

One of my favorite narratives in the Bible is when John the Baptist jumped for joy in his mother's womb when Jesus entered the room (while still in His mother's womb); indeed, John's mother, Elizabeth, was filled with the Holy Spirit in that moment (verse 41). So from the beginning, John and Jesus had a special relationship.

John prepared the way for Jesus, even going so far as to baptize tax collectors after a stern warning that they shouldn't take more than they should (Luke 3:12-13). When people asked if John was the Messiah (verse 15), he foreshadowed something Jesus Himself would later say to the woman at the well: "I baptize you with water. But one who is more powerful than I will come, the straps of whose sandals I am not worthy to untie. He will baptize you with the Holy Spirit and fire" (verse 16). John even baptized Jesus.

Despite his relationship with Jesus, John still had questions. While he was imprisoned, he sent two of his disciples to Jesus to ask Him if He was the one they had been waiting for (Luke 7:18-20). After Jesus sent His affirmative reply to John, He spoke highly of John, noting to the crowd that John was the messenger described in Malachi 3:1. John was beheaded by King Herod, and Jesus, in His sadness, sought solitude to grapple with His cousin's death. Jesus loved John, and even when John experienced a moment of doubt, Jesus responded with gentleness and proof of the miracles done in His name.

John clearly loved and admired Jesus, so much so that he died for Him. Jesus reciprocated that love for John. You might think that bridge builders don't ever wonder about the validity of their own faith, but take heart! If you've experienced doubt, you are not alone. In fact, two-thirds of Christians say they have faced doubt about God or other aspects of Christianity.[4] It is what you do with the doubt that matters. Don't try to hide it or bury it in shame. Bring it to the light. Ask questions of spiritually mature believers who can help you sort through your thoughts. Seek wisdom. And when someone comes to you with their own doubts, respond like Jesus did to John, with gentleness and evidence.

Barnabas
Lesson: Encourage others.

One of the greatest missionary teams we read about in Scripture is the one involving Paul and Barnabas. Paul, as a newly converted Christian, went to Jerusalem and was met with skepticism from other believers. After all, Paul had recently been behind the torture and killings of Christians like Stephen. Their doubt about Paul's transformation was understandable. Barnabas, however, met with and joined Paul, and he encouraged others to do the same. Although the pair parted ways later on due to a disagreement, while they were together, many people began to follow Jesus because of their efforts and faithfulness. Scripture describes Barnabas as "a good man, full of the Holy Spirit and faith" (Acts 11:24). His very name means "encourager."

As a bridge builder, we can choose to be like Barnabas—coming alongside other believers who may not yet have partners in the faith. God can use such relationships for His good as He surely did with Paul and Barnabas. Bridge builders encourage others to speak boldly and confidently proclaim the gospel. The work continues even when relationships end because that is our calling as Christ followers.

Dr. Martin Luther King Jr.
Lesson: Be willing to run into the fire to save humanity.

The Martin Luther King Jr. Memorial is located at 1964 Independence Avenue SW in Washington, DC. Its location is significant because the Civil Rights Act was passed by the US Congress in 1964. Of course, King was instrumental in the legislation, which was a result of the American civil rights movement, a crusade led in part by King. I was able to see the monument in its beginning stages in 1999, and I recall the excitement surrounding its construction. Among the 14 quotes by King inscribed at the monument is this: "Make a career of humanity. Commit yourself to the noble struggle for equal rights. You will make a greater person of yourself, a greater nation of your country, and a finer world to live in."

King spoke those words in 1959 to about 26,000 attendees at a youth march for integrated schools at the Washington Monument in Washington, DC. He started that speech noting, "As I stand here and look out upon the thousands of Negro faces, and the thousands of white faces, intermingled like the waters of a river, I see only one face—the face of the future. Yes, as I gaze upon this great historic assembly, this unprecedented gathering of young people, I cannot help thinking—that a hundred years from now the historians will be calling this not the 'beat' generation, but the generation of integration." More than 60 years have passed since that speech, but we still have work to do. There's still much room for progress. King later lamented that we are "a burning house"—and the American evangelical church is unfortunately not safe from the fire.

A seminary friend, Reverend Brandon Washington, recently wrote a book called *A Burning House* (Zondervan Reflective, 2023). In it, he suggests that integration is required for the success of American evangelicalism, that we must find a way to succeed in order to survive. He says, "Injustice, racism, classism, sexism, and a list of systemic sins are weaknesses, and as the church, we must bring the gospel to bear on them all."[5] I'm oversimplifying his proposed solutions, but ultimately, the final sentence of his book says it all: "Reorienting ourselves toward the king and his kingdom is our sole hope."[6] This somewhat echoes what King said in perhaps his most famous speech:

> ...when we let [freedom] ring from every village and every hamlet, from every state and every city, we will be able to speed up that day when all of God's children, Black men and white men, Jews and Gentiles, Protestants and Catholics, will be able to join hands and sing in the words of the old Negro spiritual: Free at last. Free at last. Thank God almighty, we are free at last.[7]

King envisioned a world where there would be no walls between races or religions. His vision reminds me of the simple saying, "Why can't we just all get along?" King proposed bridges between races and religions. He wanted to tear down the walls peacefully but powerfully too.

King saw what we needed and hoped mightily that we would one day achieve his dream: "I have a dream that one day every valley shall be exalted, every hill and mountain shall be made low, the rough places will be made plain, and the crooked places will be made straight, and the glory of the Lord shall be revealed, and all flesh shall see it together."[8] Now I realize that as fallen people, we will never reach perfect completion and unity until we are reunited with our heavenly Father in eternity. But as Christians, we must continue to strive in the hope of the gospel—being willing to run into the burning house to save humanity. We must see our brothers and sisters as just that— siblings who are deserving of gentleness, respect, truth, and love. All the while finding unity in our shared hope.

Nabeel Qureshi
Lesson: Speak truth in peace and love.

I first learned of Nabeel Qureshi in a religious pluralism class I took in seminary. About a year later, he passed away after a valiant fight against stage 4 stomach cancer. He vlogged during his final days, and I consumed each post voraciously, praying for a miracle healing (unfortunately, that was not to be). I vividly remember watching what turned out to be his final post, which was made just days before his death. In it, he said, "I think it's very important that we discuss matters of truth, but at the end of the day that is supposed to be undergirded by love and by peace. When we talk to people about our beliefs, we should do it through a lens of love."[9]

To understand the beauty behind Nabeel's words, one must look at his story. He was born into a devout Muslim-American family, and he converted to Christianity after many discussions with his friend, David Wood. Nabeel later became a Christian apologist and wrote a few books, including one featuring his testimony, titled *Seeking Allah, Finding Jesus* (Zondervan, 2015). As someone who is interested in world religions and bridge building, I was immediately drawn to Nabeel and his work.

Nabeel's words (whether in writing or in speaking) were filled with love for others, and what resonated most for me was his desire to see all people find true hope in the Savior. His ultimate goal was summed up in his final video blog: "The whole point should be to bring people together…to bring people together to the truth and not to hurt one another but to help one another."[10] In other words, he hoped for a world where bridge building was commonplace. Taking this stand wasn't easy for Nabeel. He was criticized and received death threats after his conversion. His response was simple: "You can be killed if you're following Jesus because guess what? Jesus was killed, and you're following him."[11]

Most of us won't face death threats, but we will likely encounter skeptics or those who challenge us in some way, whether it be for our faith or some other aspect of our Christian worldview. We cannot control the critics, but we do have control over the way we respond, and as Christians, it is our responsibility to respond with the truth of the gospel out of genuine love for our fellow image bearers. As Nabeel wrote in his book *No God but One*, "It is worth all suffering to receive this truth and follow him. God is more beautiful than this life itself, and the one who loves him is ready to die when death comes, not just to glorify him but to hasten to his arms. Though we will die, we will live."[12] Although Nabeel is no longer on this earth, I find joy knowing that his suffering is over, and he yet lives—safe, healthy, and secure in the arms of his Savior.

Corrie and Betsie ten Boom
Lesson: Have courage, pray, and forgive.

Fair warning: The story I'm about to tell you is probably going to make you itch, but perhaps you'll never complain about fleas again. Sisters Corrie and Betsie ten Boom and their family were part of the resistance movement against the Nazis during World War II. They created "The Hiding Place"[13] in their home—a place where they hid many Jewish refugees. It is estimated that because of the family's hard work, 800 Jewish people survived the Holocaust.[14] And then Corrie,

Betsie, and their father, Casper, were arrested. Casper and Betsie both died while imprisoned, but due to a clerical error, Corrie was released ten months after she was placed in a Nazi concentration camp. The other women her age were put to death just a week later.[15]

The ten Booms' experiences became ones of hope and inspiration worldwide when Corrie published her book *The Hiding Place* in 1971. In it, she recounts an experience involving guards and fleas. While imprisoned, Corrie and Betsie held a Bible study with other women housed in their barracks, a place where the beds were infested with fleas. And yet, much to Corrie's astonishment, Betsie gave thanks for the fleas. Yes, the fleas! And it turns out, they were a blessing in disguise. The guards avoided their barracks because of the pests, which left the women ample opportunities to pray and study Scripture together without intrusion.

The reason Corrie and Betsie are listed in this chapter as bridge builders is not because of the fleas, but for their actions and character. Despite the atrocities of what they saw and experienced, they thanked God. Even for the fleas. They prayed. They displayed Christian character, willing to put their own lives on the line for others. One biographer noted that they didn't try to convert any of the Jewish refugees they kept hidden.[16] They simply rescued them because that was the right thing to do. It was what God called them to do. They were building bridges by doing kingdom work in their own home, work that saved the lives of hundreds of people.

Ultimately, Corrie continued to be a bridge builder throughout her life. One story in particular is relevant regarding forgiveness, which is an important part of bridge building, as we'll discover in later chapters. After Corrie had given a speech about forgiveness, she was approached by a man she immediately recognized as one of the Nazi guards at her internment camp. He asked her for forgiveness, revealing that he had become a Christian and had already sought God's forgiveness. And she paused.

And still I stood there with the coldness clutching my heart. But forgiveness is not an emotion—I knew that too. Forgiveness is an act of the will, and the will can function regardless of the temperature of the heart. "Jesus, help me!" I prayed silently. "I can lift my hand. I can do that much. You supply the feeling." And so woodenly, mechanically, I thrust my hand into the one stretched out to me. And as I did, an incredible thing took place. The current started in my shoulder, raced down my arm, sprang into our joined hands. And then this healing warmth seemed to flood my whole being, bringing tears to my eyes. "I forgive you, brother!" I cried. "With all my heart!" For a long moment we grasped each other's hands, the former guard and the former prisoner. I had never known God's love so intensely as I did then.[17]

In that moment, Jesus was the bridge to healing that Corrie needed. Corrie was the bridge to healing that the former guard needed. And when those bridges were united, peace and healing could truly begin. One way to build a bridge is to extend forgiveness even (or maybe especially) when forgiveness seems impossible.

BUILDING THE BRIDGE

Learning by example can help clarify in our minds what we're shooting for, which is why I've included role models other than Jesus and Paul to help guide our way to effective bridge building. Although there are many other examples I could have used, the ones highlighted in this chapter show us that bridge building begins with our willingness to heed the call of our Creator. The bridge building lessons we learned in this chapter were:

• Take the message to the people.

- Be a willing vessel.

- Don't be afraid to ask questions.

- Encourage others.

- Be willing to run into the fire to save humanity.

- Speak truth in peace and love.

- Have courage, pray, and forgive.

As you continue to learn lessons about bridge buildings from Scripture and in modernity, notice the common threads that exist. Effective bridge builders follow the ways of Christ and exhibit a sacrificial willingness to be used by God to encourage, love, and disciple others.

In the next part of this book, we will go beyond theory and discover practical tips for doing these things well so that our bridges lead others to salvation in Christ and eternity with the Father.

QUESTIONS FOR REFLECTION AND DISCUSSION

1. What is the number one lesson you've learned so far about bridge building?

2. Reflect on some of the bridge builders mentioned in this and the preceding chapters. Is there anyone else you would add to the list, either from Scripture or today?

3. Is there a common theme you've noticed that unites the bridge builders mentioned in this book?

4. How can you encourage other Christians in their faith like Barnabas did?

5. Do you have any "fleas" in your life that you need to give thanks for?

RECOMMENDED RESOURCES

Nabeel Qureshi, *Seeking Allah, Finding Jesus: A Devout Muslim Encounters Christianity*, exp. ed. (Grand Rapids, MI: Zondervan, 2016)

Corrie ten Boom, *The Hiding Place: The Triumphant True Story of Corrie ten Boom* (New York: Bantam, 1974)

Charles Spurgeon, *The Practice of Praise* (New Kensington, PA: Whitaker House, 1995)

Jonathan Eig, *King: A Life* (New York: Farrar, Straus, and Giroux, 2023)

PART 2

BECOMING A BRIDGE BUILDER

*I firmly believe people have hitherto been a great deal too much
taken up about doctrine and far too little about practice. The word
doctrine, as used in the Bible, means teaching of duty, not theory.*

GEORGE MACDONALD[1]

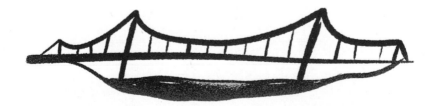

FIRM FOUNDATION 1— TRUTH

You have got to build a firm foundation on the living word of God. You have got to study it, to store it in your heart, to gain the wisdom that it gives and apply it to your life.

CALVIN W. ALLISON

The media has a lot to say about the truth, and I'm not just talking about news networks (though they may need a lesson or two in that area). From Jack Nicholson's memorable courtroom outburst in *A Few Good Men* to Black Widow explaining the subjectivity of truth to Captain America in *The Winter Soldier*, we are inundated with truth statements about truth frequently.

One needs to spend only five to ten minutes on TikTok to see that subjective truth is just as valued as objective truth, and that's a problem when it comes to worldview. Culture is confused and Christianity offers clarity. Discernment is important when dealing with truth claims, and this chapter will help you know how to stand firm in the foundational truths of Christianity.

YOUR TRUTH VERSUS MY TRUTH

I recently wrote a series of articles about the popular television show *Ancient Aliens*. The program consistently presents conspiracy theories about extraterrestrials as fact, which makes it difficult for viewers to determine what's real and what's speculation. Did aliens build the pyramids? Were extraterrestrials present on Mount Sinai?[1]

The problem is that "the more a person hears a theory presented as fact, the more likely they will begin to believe the theory is true (even if there isn't anything to prove it)."[2] This is called the illusory truth effect. Your worldview slowly changes the more times you hear something, so if you repeatedly hear that extraterrestrials built the pyramids, you're more likely to eventually believe that is true. Add in a layer of credible sources, and poof! You've got reality on a silver platter. Don't believe me? Let's look at an example involving extraterrestrials.

SpaceX founder and X owner Elon Musk made headlines in 2020 when he posted "Aliens built the pyramids, obv."[3] He's been a guest on *Ancient Aliens* and seems to have bought into at least some of the show's claims, even though he runs a space exploration company. His tweet went viral, and it even garnered him an invitation from Egypt to "discover the truth" for himself. Unfortunately, not all people who believe conspiracies will be offered an opportunity to explore the evidence face to face. We must take the time to investigate the truth claims and see whether they hold up, but how can we tell the difference between what's true and what's mere opinion offered as fact? Our culture tells us that one person's truth can be the exact opposite of another person's truth; yet, both truths are true.[4] Talk about confusing! And guess what? You don't have to give in to that lie to build bridges.

Recognize that we have a truth problem in the world, and the church and its people are falling prey to false realities. The problem is that subjective truths are being elevated to the standard of objective truths. We have to know the differences so we can spot them. Once we see the lies, we can gently offer truth as a viable alternative.

SUBJECTIVE TRUTH VERSUS OBJECTIVE TRUTH

What's your favorite color? What about your favorite pizza topping? Whatever your answer, although true for you, may not be true for me (unless you answered pink, purple, and yellow for colors and pepperoni and mushrooms for pizza toppings). Either way, your responses are subjective truths, ones that cannot be proven right or wrong. Subjective truths are often related to your experiences and feelings. Subjective truths often add color to our life, just as a commentator adds color to a baseball game. Without their opinion about how the pitcher throws or how the team is performing, all you would hear is statistics about the game itself. That could get boring!

On the other hand, it is an objective truth that I require blood pressure medication to keep my blood pressure at a healthy level, and that my friend's son needs a certain kind of medicine to keep his kidneys functioning. If either one of us stops taking our medication, barring a miracle, our numbers will head to unhealthy states. Such a claim can be proven right or wrong. Put another way, while it is an objective truth that roses are a type of flower, it is a subjective truth that they are the best kind of flower.

One of the ways we've seen the "my truth" phenomenon play out in our culture is by the way people add qualifiers at the end of objective truth statements. For example, "Eating healthy is good for *me*, but might not be for *you*." Well, no, eating healthy is good for everyone. Or "Going to church is good for *you*, but isn't for *me*." Well, no, Scripture says that coming together with other believers is good for everyone (Hebrews 10:25). We've seen this play out amidst the COVID-19 pandemic. While online church services were helpful for a time, as believers, we are meant to be together to worship collectively. Thankfully, it seems that most believers agree and have returned to in-person worship services.[5] This is objectively good news for the church and its community of believers.

One caveat that bears mentioning here: We should still take some opinions (subjective truths) seriously. If you know one of your children loves chocolate cake and hates vanilla, you're probably not going to bake them a vanilla cake for their birthday. Or if your spouse prefers a cold room at night but you prefer it a little warmer, both of you will need to take the other's opinion seriously and come to a happy medium. Keep in mind that opinions are simply that—one person's thoughts on something. Opinions can be true for you or not. But when it comes to our faith, there's no room for mere opinion. Opinions are fickle; they are sinking sand. Instead of using opinions to build our foundation, we need to build our house on a rock—that is, objective truth. If we don't, we'll be prone to cave in to any belief system that has a whiff of truth to it.

PLURALISM AND TRUTH[6]

Culture tells us to coexist, to accept (and affirm) other people's beliefs (their truths) because that's the loving thing to do. We're living in a pluralistic world—one where all worldviews (philosophies about anything and everything) are considered true. Lesslie Newbigin defined religious pluralism as "the belief that the differences between the religions are not a matter of truth and falsehood but of different perceptions of the one truth; that to speak of religious beliefs as true or false is inadmissible."[7] Unfortunately, Christians are succumbing to the pluralistic pressure.

In a 2017 survey by Barna, 23 percent of self-professed Christian respondents said morals were dependent on personal beliefs, and 15 percent said that religious beliefs are false if they offend someone.[8] *Truth* has become a dirty word. Not only that, but many Christians have also seemingly created their own blend of Christianity—a mixture of beliefs, biblical or not, that suits their own needs. Perhaps this is why we see so many Christians falling prey to New Age ideologies like astrology, reincarnation, and karma—truth is said to be found in the stars and through Eastern religious practices and beliefs.[9]

There are obviously differences in religions, but the chasm isn't so wide that a bridge can't close the gap, at least in the name of peacekeeping. However, despite our desire to live in shalom with others, we must not deny the truth when challenged about our beliefs. We've become Peter after Jesus' crucifixion, but we're not being warned by a crowing rooster. Yet the warning signs are there. Let's courageously defend our beliefs with the understanding that others may reject them. Rejection is a choice, and although we may disagree, we can still maintain peace with one another as encouraged to do so in Romans 12:18 ("be at peace with all men"), yet know that there may come times when those who reject us will do so with hostility. As we continue to build bridges, perhaps the truth will prevail. Perhaps not. Don't stop trusting the Lord to do His mighty work, for He is the path to eternal rescue and reconciliation with the Father.

THE NEW AGE IN THE PRESENT AGE[10]

Thanks in part to social media (specifically TikTok), what once was old (the New Age movement) is trending again. It's not just catchy tunes like Enya's "Sail Away" or Hair's "Age of Aquarius." It's more than incense and hippies. The New Age movement is a worldview that permeated the 1960s through 1980s but still thrives today—it's sort of a mash-up of Eastern religions like Hinduism, Sikhism, and Buddhism. Crystals with alleged powers, astrology for signs in the stars, psychics for magical insight, and the TikTok trend #witchtok[11] are all popular, and we're seeing an uptick in New Age beliefs among Millennials and Gen Zers.[12]

There's a growing hunger for deeper meaning in life, and the youngest generations are finding it in mindfulness and metaphysical spirituality rather than in Christianity. It's essential that we understand where the trends are so we can build bridges that actually help lead young people to truth, not whims of man built on sinking sand. Satan "prowls around like a roaring lion looking for someone to devour" (1 Peter 5:8), but you need only to "resist the devil, and he will flee from you" (James 4:7). By understanding the New Age worldview, we can be on alert for the potential snags it creates in truth.

New Agers are pluralists and generally believe in monism, a fancy word for "everything is one" (don't confuse this with monotheism, the belief in one God). They also usually believe that all is God, including humanity. It's exactly the sort of belief that Paul was telling the Christians in Rome to stay away from in Romans 1:25. New Agers also tend to believe that all religions are one (called syncretism). That muddies the waters of truth, doesn't it? Reincarnation and karma are essential for New Agers, too, and according to them, Jesus was a mere teacher, not God.

Taking all of that into account, it's clear that Christianity and the New Age movement are not aligned. And guess what? People are buying what the New Age movement is selling, and some don't even realize it. After I wrote an article about New Age for Mama Bear Apologetics, I had a friend reach out to me and let me know that she just discovered she's a New Ager. Your friends, relatives, and neighbors are being entrenched in New Age thinking through films, books, and podcasts and may not know it. And slowly, their beliefs are being transformed by falsehood rather than the renewal of their minds in Christ Jesus (Romans 12:2).

In his book *A Crash Course on the New Age Movement*, Elliot Miller suggests that "no Christian is immune from exposure to New Age influence."[13] Truth isn't fragile, but our minds (and especially our hearts) are. We need to be firm in the truth and not compromise to be trendy. Do not "turn away from listening to the truth and wander off into myths" (2 Timothy 4:4 ESV).

CONSPIRACY THEORIES

I recently spent some time in Roswell, New Mexico. Although we enjoyed visiting an alien-themed museum and laughed a lot, I was also struck by the realization that many people who live there and visit there believe wholeheartedly that extraterrestrials crashed there decades ago. It's a conspiracy theory born in the 1940s that survives today.

Conspiracy theories spread like wildfire, especially on the internet. From the moon landing being called a hoax to the assassination of US president John F. Kennedy not happening to various sightings of Bigfoot and the Loch Ness monster, conspiracy theories are as interesting as they are unbelievable. With groups like QAnon making waves in recent years, conspiracy theories have been on the rise, and they are entering churches with gusto. A 2021 survey from Lifeway Research found that 49 percent of US-based Protestant pastors have frequently heard conspiracy theories repeated by church members.[14] And it is not just Americans that are influenced by conspiracy theories.[15] The internet age is rife with them,[16] and modern-day bridge builders need to know what to say when confronted with them.

Truth is the only right answer. If we don't know the answer, it's okay to admit that. We can even admit that some conspiracy theories sound like they could be true. But we also need to base what we say on evidence. If you have a friend or family member who subscribes to conspiracy theories, do some research on your own about the specifics they believe. Then, if you think it would be helpful, talk with them. Ask questions and show them what you've found. Don't be an inadvertent purveyor of falsehood, letting theories take over truth.

ARTIFICIAL INTELLIGENCE

I've spent a lot of time lately thinking about Artificial Intelligence (AI). I even teach a lesson about generative AI in one of my writing courses. As an author, I've wondered about the impact of AI on the written word. Will AI write authors out of the script, so to speak? Thankfully, it seems like authors are not pegged for death quite yet, but AI presents other problems—namely, how do we know whether what we are seeing is real? Recently, an X profile[17] that went viral featured a woman claiming to be a former field organizer for President Joe Biden. She had more than 130,000 followers and posted all sorts of racist and otherwise hurtful statements, garnering retweets and comments from even some of my own friends. We believed she was real. Then the news broke that the account was AI-generated, even down to the profile photo. This is the kind of stuff that makes people concerned about AI, but I believe it should make us more concerned about preserving truth.

Truth is being manipulated and twisted by AI, and some of us can't identify when we're being duped because AI appears to be so authentic. As Christians, we need to be mindful of what we repeat and share. Just like with conspiracy theories, our desire should be to spread truth and truth alone. When we discover that we've shared unreliable information online or in person, we need to apologize for doing so. We need to try to fix the mistake because our responsibility is to be honest about the evidence we have, not to be opportunists who seek more likes and shares because a so-called news item is sexy. If you do get fooled by AI, own up to it and note just how important it is to verify, verify, and verify again in this digital age.

One final note: Using AI isn't wrong (so long as we aren't calling AI's work our own), and in many cases, having a conversation with something like ChatGPT can be fun. But we shouldn't use AI at the expense of truth. Don't use it to cheat, lie, or manipulate others into believing something that's not true. And be mindful that others aren't necessarily being as honest as they should be about their use of it. Be on guard.

THE WAY, THE TRUTH, AND THE LIFE

Shortly before His arrest and crucifixion, Jesus gathered His disciples to explain how He would be going away for a time but would later come back and take them to be with Him. Thomas (bless him and his truth-seeking questions) asked how they would know the way if they didn't know where they were going. "Jesus answered, 'I am the way and the truth and the life. No one comes to the Father except through me'" (John 14:6). In other words, Jesus is the bridge between this life and reconciliation and eternity with our Creator. I can't think of a firmer foundation than the Savior of the world.

Although I already spent a whole chapter talking about Jesus as a bridge builder, I want to call out one more lesson we can learn from the King of kings and Lord of lords.

Jesus

Lesson: Balance truth and love.

Time and time again, we see this lesson played out in Jesus' life. He was truly the master of "speaking the truth in love" (Ephesians 4:15). Let's look at the way Jesus responded to Thomas after His resurrection. The other disciples had told Thomas Jesus had risen from the dead, but Thomas said he wouldn't buy what they were selling unless he touched Jesus' wounds for himself. When Jesus showed up a week later, Jesus gave Thomas what he needed to believe.

> Though the doors were locked, Jesus came and stood among them and said, "Peace be with you!" Then he said to Thomas, "Put your finger here; see my hands. Reach out your hand and put it into my side. Stop doubting and believe." Thomas said to him, "My Lord and my God!" Then Jesus told him, "Because you have seen me, you have believed; blessed are those who have not seen and yet have believed" (John 20:26-29).

What's most striking about this interaction is that Jesus didn't laugh at Thomas's doubts or make him the laughingstock of the disciples. He didn't use Thomas as a punchline. No, Jesus responded with truth *and* love. Thomas went on to spread the gospel throughout the land, and tradition tells us he went to India, where he was likely martyred. Jesus is the Way, the Truth, and the Life, just as He claimed to be. He was quick to reveal the truth, knowing that even the best of us may need proof that goes beyond personal testimony to believe what we do.

This lesson shouldn't come as a surprise for Jesus followers. We should already know that our task is to show people genuine love as an outpouring of the truth that our faith is grounded in. Matt Brown wrote an excellent book called *Truth Plus Love*, and he eloquently sums up our mission in this way: "The kind of love that can change the world is an expressly Christian kind of love. It is a love for others that can only be fueled and motivated by the cross, shed blood, and resurrection of Jesus Christ."[18] Brown reminds his readers that by walking in truth and love the way that Jesus did, "we will influence others for the sake of the gospel."[19] The gospel is what motivated those in the early church to sacrifice all they could (even their own lives) so that more people could find the peace offered through Jesus Christ alone.

SHALOM, SHALOM

Shortly after Jesus assured His disciples that He was the way, the truth, and the life, He said, "Peace I leave with you; my peace I give you. I do not give to you as the world gives. Do not let your hearts be troubled and do not be afraid" (John 14:27). It was typical in Jewish culture to greet someone with peace (shalom). *Shalom* means much more than simply the absence of conflict or war. It is more than flashing a peace sign and hoping for no war.

One year around Christmastime, I taught about peace at my church. In the weeks leading up to the talk, I studied a lot about what peace means in the context of Scripture. Ultimately, shalom is a genuine concern for the well-being of others. Shalom is wholeness. It is flourishing. It is completeness. So when Jesus left His peace with us, He was offering us completeness and wholeness in Him. He is, after all, the Prince of Peace (Isaiah 9:6). He is the bridge to harmony with God. Paul described Jesus in this way:

> He himself is our peace, who has made the two groups one and has destroyed the barrier, the dividing wall of hostility, by setting aside in his flesh the law with its commands and regulations. His purpose was to create in himself one new humanity out of the two, thus making peace, and in one body to reconcile both of them to God through the cross, by which he put to death their hostility. He came and preached peace to you who were far away and peace to those who were near. For through him we both have access to the Father by one Spirit (Ephesians 2:14-18).

Once we've realized that we are incomplete without Jesus, we're on the path to peace—a bridge, so to speak. Jesus is the bridge that holds us together with the Father. He reconciles us to God. *Reconciliation* is a ten-dollar word for a renewed coming together. Because of what Jesus did—coming down to earth as fully human and fully God, dying on the cross, rising from the dead three days later, and ascending to heaven—we can be made complete. We can be made whole. Cornelius Plantinga described shalom in this way:

> *universal flourishing, wholeness, and delight*—a rich state of affairs in which natural needs are satisfied and natural gifts fruitfully employed, a state of affairs that inspires

joyful wonder as its Creator and Savior opens doors and
welcomes the creatures in whom he delights. Shalom, in
other words, is the way things ought to be.[20]

How it ought to be. Before the fall. Before sin. Unfortunately,
the reality is that we live in a fallen world. Thankfully, though, Jesus
came to set things right. This is the hope within us. This is the foundation on which we stand. It will not falter. It will not fail. It will
not cease in the face of culture wars. Culture is yearning for completion, for wholeness, for shalom. And Jesus is the firm foundation on
which we can build a bridge to help people reach everlasting shalom.

DON'T LEAVE YOUR ARMOR AT HOME

Stand firm then, with the belt of truth buckled around
your waist, with the breastplate of righteousness in place,
and with your feet fitted with the readiness that comes
from the gospel of peace. In addition to all this, take up
the shield of faith, with which you can extinguish all the
flaming arrows of the evil one. Take the helmet of salvation
and the sword of the Spirit, which is the word of God
(Ephesians 6:14-17).

How do you get dressed in the morning? I'll admit that I usually
don't give my clothing choices much thought because I've never been
one to care much about fashion. I know that's not true for everyone;
some people take great care to consider what they wear. No matter
what our level of attention to our physical clothing, we should definitely consider our spiritual clothing, or the armor of God.

The armor of God equips us for all we do as Christians—the
belt of *truth*, the breastplate of *righteousness*, the shoes of *shalom*, the
shield of *faith*, the helmet of *salvation*, and the sword of the *Spirit*. As

a bridge builder, you should never leave home without your armor. You wouldn't go fishing without a fishing pole or canoeing without a paddle, would you? Notice that the armor is mostly defensive, not offensive. God's armor protects you from the "flaming arrows of the evil one" (Ephesians 6:16).

You may not be in a physical battle against Satan and his minions, but you're certainly in a spiritual one. This is not a battle with the people of this world, so you don't get free reign to attack people. Your battle is against false ideas and false narratives about Jesus, not people whom God made in His image. The way you use your armor will affect those around you. Don't wield truth as a weapon; use it as a life-giving salve.

SO, WHAT'S THE TRUTH?

We're admonished in 1 Peter 3:15 to be ready to give a defense for "the reason for the hope that you have." Our hope is truth, the message of the gospel. Jesus, the only Son of God, came to earth, fully God and fully human, engaged in a teaching ministry for three years, was crucified and died, was resurrected on the third day, and 40 days later, ascended to heaven. He died so that we may live. His death and resurrection represent the satisfaction of the debt of our sins. That's the hope within us. That is what should get us going in the morning, motivating us to build bridges, bring light to the darkness, shed truth on lies, and spread love and truth everywhere we go. Don't let the truth get watered down by the things of this world; instead, remember that "you were washed, you were sanctified, you were justified in the name of the Lord Jesus Christ and by the Spirit of our God" (1 Corinthians 6:11).

The Truth Saves Lives

Truth can be difficult. It can be painful. However, the truth about truth is that it saves lives. This is why sticking with the truth of the gospel message is so important, especially in light of today's culture. Douglas Groothuis summed this up best in his book *Christian Apologetics*:

> Religion is wide, but truth is narrow. Truth captures reality in statements, and any statement that fails that task is erroneous. Error in religion is no small thing, and it can be a matter of eternal consequence if that error be egregious enough. The end of true religion must be truth, saving and flaming truth.[21]

Bridge builders understand the relationship between truth and love—you shouldn't have one without the other. Because, as Groothuis recognizes, whether we speak truth can have eternal consequences for those we love.

We should also be aware that the truth, while it can set people free, it can also require a high price of us. It may cause rifts between family members and friends. It may result in shunning. It could very well result in death. When we share the truth with someone, we can't forget the impact it can have, both positive and negative. Don't take the responsibility of truth-telling lightly. Instead, navigate it with gentleness, humility, and love.

How's Your Oxygen Mask?

How can you ensure that your bridge-building efforts are based on a firm foundation, a requirement for all sustainable bridges? You want to make sure your own foundation is sufficient before you try to help someone else with their foundation. When you fly on an airline, before you take off, the flight attendants give a pre-flight safety demonstration. Part of that demonstration is about oxygen masks, and adults are warned to put on their own masks before assisting any children around them. This is because if the adults run out of oxygen, they will be of little use to the children they are trying to help.

The same goes for building bridges. If your own foundation is unstable or shaky, it will be difficult to help build a strong foundation for someone else. To ensure your faith foundation is firm, here are a few things you can do:

1. *Check your spiritual practices.* Do you worship God daily? Do you pray? How about church attendance and Bible study? How often do you open the Word of God?

2. *Check your lifestyle choices.* Do you fill your mind with pure thoughts through the media you consume or the books you read? Are you engaging in positive relationships both in person and online? How often do you participate in activities that perhaps might not be in the best interest of you or your family?

3. *Check your reasoning skills.* Can you spot fallacies (faulty arguments)? When's the last time you read a resource about logic? What are you doing to gird up truth in your life so that you can spot falsehood?

Although these self-checks aren't foolproof, they are steps in the right direction. They will help ensure that your faith foundation is secure and efficient, even when you are challenged by other worldviews or you get into cultural debates. I would encourage you to choose one check from each category to work on in your life, or maybe there are other checks you need to implement that aren't listed above. Maybe you need to cut out certain television shows from your nighttime routine, or you need to pray more. Maybe you should start using a Bible reading plan or stop engaging uncivilly with people on the internet. Whatever you require, "do your best to present yourself to God as one approved, a worker who does not need to be ashamed and who correctly handles the word of truth" (2 Timothy 2:15).

BUILDING THE BRIDGE

As we learned in chapter 2, bridges require solid foundations, or they will crumble. Truth is an absolutely essential aspect of the foundation required for effective bridge building. Without truth, we are nothing. Our truth is found in our Savior, and with our knowledge of the redemption found through His death and resurrection, we can combat the lies of the enemy, often wrapped up in ideals found in New Age thinking, witchcraft, conspiracy theories, and so many other things found in today's world. We need to be on guard, but we don't need to live in fear. Our Lord has equipped us with His armor, which protects us as we combat the lies of the enemy. Moving forward will take courage and a persevering hope. Yet we find our confidence in Him, the one who saved us. Once we have firmly established ourselves on the truth, we can work on the second foundational requirement of bridge building: friendship.

QUESTIONS FOR REFLECTION AND DISCUSSION

1. Have you ever believed something that you later found out was false? How did you react when you discovered the truth?

2. What's the difference between subjective truth and objective truth? Give an example of both.

3. Explain pluralism as simply as you can. How can we be tolerant of other belief systems without affirming them?

4. Give an example of a time when you were able to share the truth with someone and showed them love at the same time. What was their response?

5. What part of the armor of God do you value the most? What part do you need to remember to wear?

RECOMMENDED RESOURCES

Matt Brown, *Truth Plus Love: The Jesus Way to Influence* (Grand Rapids, MI: Zondervan, 2019)

Paul Copan and Benjamin B. DeVan, "Religious Pluralism," in *The Popular Handbook of World Religions*, ed. Daniel J. McCoy (Eugene, OR: Harvest House, 2021)

Nathaniel Bluedorn & Hans Bluedorn, *The Fallacy Detective* (Quartz Hill, CA: Christian Logic, 2015)

Carmen LaBerge, *Speak the Truth: How to Bring God Back into Every Conversation* (Washington, DC: Regnery Faith, 2017)

FIRM FOUNDATION 2— FRIENDSHIP

*Friendship is no optional extra life feature we might get talked
into by an eager salesman. It's vital to our flourishing.*[1]

REBECCA MCLAUGHLIN

riendship. Typically, we find our circle of friends through shared
interests and life stages, whether that's the same church, school,
workplace, playground, or phase of life. Many times, our relationships grow as we grow, and typically the pattern looks something like
this: we are kids, we become adults, we are single, then we're married, then we have young children, and so on. Sometimes a friendship
doesn't fit this exact mold (I met my best friend when our families
were already established and we were well into our thirties, but we
were both attending seminary, so we definitely had shared interests).
For most of us, our circle of friends is usually made up of people with
the same values and ideals too. But there are exceptions.

Every once in a while, we hear about a great friendship that tran-
scends ideology. One such example is the friendship between former
US Supreme Court Justices Antonin Scalia (d. 2016) and Ruth Bader
Ginsburg (d. 2020). Scalia was appointed to the Court by Repub-
lican president Ronald Reagan, while Ginsburg was appointed by
Democratic president Jimmy Carter. They had known each other

for years beforehand, when they served together on the US Court of Appeals for the DC circuit. Ginsburg and Scalia had common backgrounds and shared passions: They both grew up in New York and loved opera, teaching, and wine. They were truly friends. Ginsburg went so far as to call them "best buddies."[2]

Yet Scalia and Ginsburg were quite different ideologically. They had wildly varied perspectives on hot-button issues like abortion. Still, they respected one another. Scalia called their relationship a "mutual improvement society."[3] That is, they worked well together because they knew they were both trying to do the best they could to solve the issues presented to them. Ginsburg later quoted Scalia to explain their unlikely friendship: "I attack ideas. I don't attack people. Some very good people have some very bad ideas."[4]

Despite their distinct views, they cared for one another and seemed to look out for each other. They even went so far as to help each other create better arguments for one another. One such example was when Ginsburg wrote the majority opinion for *U.S. v. Virginia* (518 U.S. 515) in 1996. Before it was published, Scalia shared his unpublished dissent with her, and of it she said, "My final draft was much improved, thanks to Justice Scalia's searing criticism."[5] Ginsburg and Scalia made a choice to be friends, even though on the face of things, that shouldn't have worked out because of their disagreements on some very big issues. Their friendship was unusual, to be sure, but why should it have been? To quote Rodney King, "Can we all get along?"[6]

You might remember from chapter 2 that one of the three keys to a stable bridge is a firm foundation. Of course, as Christians, our firm foundation is truth (see chapter 8), but there's more. A second foundational element that is essential to effective bridge building is friendship—genuine, in-the-trenches friendship. Finding people you can rely on and who can rely on you. Who you can support and who can support you. Who will tell you the truth even when it hurts, and who expect you to do the same.

This chapter will help you with your people skills because bridge building is all about people. Some of us need to brush up on our people skills because relationships are at the core of bridge building. We've already learned some lessons from the Bible and modernity about how to build bridges—that is, we've filled our minds with theory. Now it is time to get practical and put our learning into motion.

FRIENDSHIP IS GOOD FOR YOU

It's true—friendship is good for your heart, your mind, and your body. In a 2023 study, researchers determined that the number of friends one has, as well as the amount of time friends spend with one another, has a positive effect on a person's well-being.[7] Further, friendships can help keep you healthy—"adults with strong social connections have a reduced risk of many significant health problems, including depression, high blood pressure and an unhealthy body mass index."[8] The variables that ensure our friendships contribute to a healthy well-being include maintenance of friendship, perceived mattering, personal sense of uniqueness, friendship quality, satisfaction of basic psychological needs, and subjective vitality.[9] That is, we're healthier if our friendships make us feel valued, special, and wanted. The trick is attaining friendships and keeping them.

The global COVID-19 pandemic certainly made us aware of how important connection and friendship truly are in that it exposed our need for closeness with other people (yes, even the introverts among us!). As the early days and weeks of the pandemic progressed, I got restless and wanted to see our friends. Isolation is not good for the soul; even virtual connection was a good alternative to nothing at all.

Despite the isolation Americans felt, it seems that they still found ways to stay connected, and roughly half of respondents to the 2021 American Perspectives Survey reported that they made a new friend during the pandemic.[10] Unfortunately, many people also lost friends during that time, and loneliness among adults seems to have increased since 2020. That matters because people who are lonely are more likely to die prematurely.[11] Our bodies and minds need connection in order to thrive and survive. Knowing this, we should prioritize friendships just as we prioritize healthy food (yes, you should prioritize that) and physical exercise (yep, that too).

HOW DO WE MAKE FRIENDS?

So, we know friendship is good for us, but you might be asking yourself, especially if you're an introvert, *How do we make friends as adults?* I can already hear you introverts groaning. Know that I feel your pain. I'm about as introverted as you can get on the MBTI[12] scale. Being an introvert presents some potential struggles in the friendship-building department, but not all is lost. There's hope for us because friendships can be formed in so many ways, including through music, sports, volunteering, church, work, and even online.[13] I won't highlight all the ways we can make friends, but let's talk about a few so we can get the ball rolling in the right direction.

Music. We saw how music bridged people together across the planet during the early stages of the COVID-19 pandemic when a video showing Italians on their balconies singing their national anthem together went viral. In fact, during that time, many videos of neighborhoods coming together through song went viral. They inspired hope and joy and unity in a time of uncertainty and sadness and loneliness.

Music brings people of all sorts together, making it a perfect helpmate for making friends. For example, I was at a Skillet concert in the spring of 2023. In the middle of their set, band frontman John Cooper had us look around the room at each other. He told us about how music brings people together and that the concert was full of people from many different backgrounds with a variety of beliefs.

And yet we were all there, together in one place, not thinking about any of that. Rather, we enjoyed the show together.

Even though we didn't make lifelong friends that night, it's not completely unheard of for someone to meet their best friend at a concert.[14] So, the next time you're lining up for a performance by your favorite musical artist, look around and strike up a conversation with someone. That show could be the bridge that brings you together.

Sports. If you're a sports fan, you might think that it's obvious that sports events bring people together. I remember a group of girls and I getting together on February 14, 2003,[15] for a Galentine's Day night—spaghetti dinner and a hockey game afterward. We cheered on the team and high-fived others in the crowd each time the home team scored a goal. Our friendships were strengthened that day through our shared experience at the hockey game. I also eventually married one of the hockey players we saw on the ice that night, so really, sports events do bring people together.

Of course, playing a sport on a team will most likely yield friendships,[16] but sports are a team-building activity even when we aren't the ones on the field.[17] We're a united front against the opposition, at least for a few hours. We see this in local sports—I think our entire town went to the state championship and watched our high school football team win their second title in a row. We see this in professional sports too. Who doesn't rally together to cheer on their favorite teams at the Stanley Cup Finals or the Super Bowl? We see it globally too—we try our best to learn the rules of obscure sports like synchronized swimming, super giant slalom, and dressage so we can cheer on our country at the Olympics. Sports are more than just a game—they are a unifying activity upon which we can build fantastic, lifelong friendships.

Online. I'm here to tell you that despite what the masses may say, it is possible to have genuine friendships with people online. Generally, online friendships will not be as deep as in-person friendships;

however, research indicates that the longer a friendship persists, the more closely aligned online friendships become with in-person friendships.[18] In other words, the more we spend time with people, whether in person or online, the deeper our relationships will be.

Furthermore, if people bolster their existing in-person friendships with online interaction, a deeper relationship will likely result.[19] So, that group chat you have with your work friends? That's probably beneficial for you in the long run. A word of caution here, though: Online friendships should not replace your in-person friendships because your real-life friends will be better for your subjective well-being; that is, you'll see yourself in a better light if you have more in-person friendships than online ones, which means you'll likely have more confidence to pursue deeper conversations and attachments.[20] Bridge building is better in real life, but that doesn't mean it can't happen virtually. Either way, be genuine, show love, and exhibit Christian character.

PRIORITIZING FRIENDSHIP

One reason we often don't make new friends as adults is that we choose to spend our time doing other things. We simply don't place enough importance on socializing, and instead, we prioritize things like entertainment.[21] And even when we do eventually make friends, it can be tough to keep the friendships strong due to factors like distance, romantic relationships, and employment changes, to name a few.[22] YouTuber Hank Green once said this about making friends as adults:

> When you're young, you make friends easily because you find it very easy to value other people...But as we get older, and we're exposed to more people who might not be worth being friends with, we start to value other things...*We're*

less likely to value other people and less likely to be quickly valued by others.[23]

It comes down to value, regarding something as worthy of our time. In this context, friendship. Are we willing to set aside other things for the sake of friendship?

Given how busy people are today, it is no wonder that friendship often gets set aside because of obligations, errands, and dare I say it, self-care. Those things all matter, but we need to find time to invest in our friendships too. One simple way to do this is to schedule dates with your friends. I have a virtual coffee date with my friend Heather several times a month. We've done this for years now, and it is virtual because we live in different states (and time zones!). But getting together with her for coffee over Zoom is one of the highlights of my week, every week. Sometimes we cry together. Other times we laugh. And sometimes we just talk about the books we're reading, or the television shows we're watching. There's no agenda to what we discuss—we're simply there together, valuing each other's company.

We all need to have a Ginsburg-Scalia view of friendship, which matters in the greater context of our story as humanity. We, as Christians especially, need to approach friendships differently, recognizing how good it is to be truly loved and valued *by* others and how good it is to do the same *for* others. "You want to make friends as an adult," Green explains. "You have to figure out how to really value other people and to get them to believe that it matters how much you value them."[24]

HOW DO WE KEEP FRIENDS?

Of course, prioritizing friendships is important for keeping friendships. But once we do, what's next? That question is a bit more difficult to answer because I think the topic merits an entire book or two (surely more than that have been written). I keep talking about how friendships need to be genuine, but what does that look like in the real world?

In an adaptation of Dale Carnegie's bestselling book *How to Win Friends & Influence People*, the authors adjust his original work to apply in our time, the digital age. Part 3 is called "How to Merit and Maintain Others' Trust." The recommendations include

- avoiding arguments,
- avoiding accusations about wrongness in opinion,
- admitting mistakes,
- finding common ground, and
- being empathetic.[25]

These may seem obvious, but they are easily forgotten in the throes of relationships, especially in the tone-deaf online world. This makes it all the more important that we strive to lead with moral Christian character in words, thoughts, and deeds. I say thoughts here because even though thoughts often go unspoken, they influence the way we behave. Also, Jesus said our thoughts matter: "'What comes out of a person is what defiles them. *For it is from within, out of a person's heart, that evil thoughts come*—sexual immorality, theft, murder, adultery, greed, malice, deceit, lewdness, envy, slander, arrogance and folly. All these evils come from inside and defile a person'" (Mark 7:20-23, emphasis added). The way we think about others impacts the way we treat them. Instead of hateful or cruel thoughts, "whatever is true, whatever is noble, whatever is right, whatever is pure, whatever is lovely, whatever is admirable—if anything is excellent or praiseworthy—think about such things" (Philippians 4:8). Keeping your thoughts pure can help you keep your friendships pure and wonderful and true.

Be a Peacemaker

I recently rewatched *Legally Blonde* (I'm a blonde lawyer [except when I dye my hair red] who is also a member of a sorority, so I'm probably the exact right audience for the film), and I was struck by a specific scene involving two key characters, Elle and Vivian. If you're not familiar with the plot, Vivian and Elle didn't get along because Vivian was dating Elle's ex-boyfriend. They both had preconceived notions about one another, and their first impressions were awful. There was a lot to overcome, and there were some terrible scenes in which Vivian tried to embarrass Elle, including one where she told Elle that a party was a costume party (it wasn't, and Elle wore a provocative costume). Yeah, it was embarrassing.

Despite Vivian's actions, Elle continued to be kind to Vivian. She was frustrated, of course, but she was also nice. Elle was gracious—she was a peacemaker. Late in the film, Vivian and Elle were interns at the same law firm. They both stepped off opposite elevators on their first day, and there was a moment of awkwardness. Elle broke the silence by complimenting Vivian. Vivian smiled, said thanks, and replied with a kind word of her own for Elle. This was the beginning of a change in their relationship.

Elle was a bridge builder, despite encountering trials. She was a peacemaker. A friendship with Vivian wasn't forged right away, but over time, walls were torn down, and foundations were laid for true relationship. Vivian stepped out of her comfort zone (uptight, unrelenting, and downright mean) and allowed herself to see Elle's value as a human and as a friend. Sometimes we need to see past our own world and step into someone else's for the possibility of friendship to become reality.

Remember when Finnick Odair gently reminded Katniss Everdeen who the real enemy is in the climactic scene in *Catching Fire*? People aren't our enemies. Instead, our enemy is found in the spiritual realm. So how can we continue to build positive and true friendships rather than burn bridges as fierce rivals? Peacemaking can be a step in the right direction. After all, "Blessed are the peacemakers, for they will be called children of God" (Matthew 5:9).

Get Out of the Echo Chamber

One simple way to make friends is to step outside of your echo chamber. That might make you feel like throwing this book across the room, but hear me out. I'm not saying that you shouldn't have friends who are like you, but I agree with the old proverb that variety is the spice of life. Here's why: It is easy to believe the rest of the world agrees with you and that your opinion is always correct if you've put yourself in an echo chamber. This is true online and in real life. Psychologist Chris Crandall says it is beneficial to be lovingly challenged:

> Friends are for comfort, taking it easy, relaxing, not being challenged—and those are good things. But you can't have only that need. You also need new ideas, people to correct you when you're loony. If you hang out only with people who are loony like you, you can be out of touch with the big, beautiful diverse world.[26]

Are you intentionally seeking out friends who are different than you? My circle of friends on X is full of all types of people: different races, different religions (or no religion), different socioeconomic statuses, different ideologies. It works for me, and it helps to expose me to different perspectives on all types of issues, from news events to political elections to who prefers cats over dogs.

Boundaries can be helpful and are important in some cases (see chapter 13) but second-guess yourself the next time you reach for the block button. In most cases, it's probably more helpful to mute, unfollow, or snooze. That will keep the window open on the relationship, allow for reconciliation, and help you to avoid an awkward "re-friend" situation later on when things have cooled off.

Find Common Ground

There's a coffee shop in my area called Common Grounds. I love the double meaning in the shop's name. You're going to a coffee shop, so obviously there will be coffee grounds, but you are probably sharing the space with people you've never met, and you're on common ground (the coffee shop). How many times have you been at a coffee shop and asked someone what they were working on or what they were reading? Connecting is a little less difficult when you're on common ground.

Whether you find yourself at your kid's soccer practice or the place you love to get your caffeine fix, don't overcomplicate it. "Ask people what they did over the weekend, what they hope to do for their next vacation, or what books they've recently read," suggests Carnegie, "and you'll find something compelling and revealing about their goals, their dreams."[27] You don't need to stretch the truth to find connection and common ground—go with what you see from the outset. Bridge building is best when you make an effort to get to know other people, and when they, in turn, desire to learn more about you.

If, after some time, you realize you don't have much in common after all, focus on what you do like. Not every person you meet will become your friend, but that doesn't mean you can't show them the love of Christ in the moments you do spend with one another. Common ground can help you keep the conversation going.

Don't Waver on Truth

Recently, I saw a post on social media that said, "If standing up for truth burns a bridge, I have matches." As Christians, we shouldn't celebrate burning bridges with people God wants to call His own (everyone). Yes, the truth is important, and we shouldn't sacrifice it on the altar of common ground. No, you shouldn't waver even when you are pushed to change your beliefs. But remember, "our struggle is not against flesh and blood, but against the rulers, against the authorities, against the powers of this dark world and against the spiritual forces of evil in the heavenly realms" (Ephesians 6:12). Truth might burn a bridge, but we shouldn't set out to light it on fire.

When Paul reasoned from the Scriptures with Jewish people and Gentiles, he didn't set out to burn down the house. Rather, he wanted to destroy the spiritual strongholds that had taken root in his culture. He wanted to loosen those bonds with power from heaven, the power given to him by the Holy Spirit. If our sole intent is to tear down bridges with truth, we've lost the mark.

Scalia and Ginsburg didn't waver on their beliefs to sustain their friendship. They interpreted the law differently from one another, and they both chose to stand their ground. Though they sustained their beliefs, they didn't waver on their friendship. There's a fine line between acceptance and affirmation, my friend. As Christians, our truth is found in Scripture. The truth is our Savior. It's true that a failure to waver may result in a loss of friendship. It might also strengthen it.

Unfortunately, it is countercultural to stand up for the truth because our society has elevated affirmation over candor, all in the name of love. The problem with that, according to Christian apologist Amy Hall, is "the truth has to be the highest thing. There is no adjusting the truth for a higher goal because if God is truth, we can't fudge on the truth."[28] As a bridge builder, your highest goal should be to speak the truth in all circumstances. The good news is that the best friendships are developed with integrity and trust. How we talk about truth and our feelings and our beliefs is the key. I believe this is why Peter emphasized gentleness and respect in 1 Peter 3:15. People won't be friends with you if they don't like or respect you. Respect is earned. Trust is earned. Make yourself worthy of friendship. That might result in adjusting your own views about things or in a change of worldview among your friends. As actress Amy Poehler once said, "Find a group of people who challenge and inspire you; spend a lot of time with them, and it will change your life." Or theirs.

FRIENDS PICK UP THE PIECES

Sometimes we need friends to help us get to the finish line. We may not even see the ending. One such example of this occurred in connection with the Brooklyn Bridge. Emily Warren Roebling was an engineer who lived in the late 1800s. Her father-in-law, John A. Roebling, designed the Brooklyn Bridge, and her husband, Washington Roebling, was the bridge's chief engineer. Emily's father-in-law died of tetanus, and her husband was bedridden after developing decompression sickness. Yet Emily carried on with a mission to complete the Brooklyn Bridge. She also worked hard to keep her husband on as chief engineer, despite his illness. She became the bridge between her husband and everyone else, interacting with politicians and workmen to keep the bridge progressing.

On the day the Brooklyn Bridge opened, Emily was the first to cross it, to cheers from the bridge workers.[29] She helped pick up the pieces when her husband could no longer complete the project on his own. She didn't seek recognition for her actions; instead, she continued to lift up her husband to ensure he would continue to hold the title of chief engineer.

As Christian bridge builders, we need to recognize the pain and heartache that can come to those who leave a different religion or simply proclaim faith in Jesus. It's risky for them because some religions shun the deconverted. This can result in a complete overhaul of a person's life. Their life, as they have known it, crumbles. When a person leaves a cult, for example, everything they have known as true has been completely shattered. They are left to pick up the pieces, often alone, because their family will no longer have anything to do with the so-called apostate.

I have friends who have left specific religions whose family will no longer speak with them. Shunning is meant to teach that person a lesson, but far too often, it results in tragedy like depression and suicide.[30] The risk is great, and we need to be willing to walk alongside our friends as they make difficult, life-changing decisions. Sometimes we'll need to pick up the pieces for them and carry the torch. Good friends do that selflessly, without ulterior motives. Be the hope when a friend has none.

THE CHRIST EFFECT

In the last several months, I've learned a lot about soccer (football to everyone outside of the US; I'll use the terms interchangeably), and it is not because my daughters play the sport (one dabbled, but now she's dancing). I've learned about soccer from television and YouTube. It all started when one of my co-workers suggested that I watch *Welcome to Wrexham*.[31] The docuseries highlights the journey of the UK football club, Wrexham, particularly after it was purchased by actor friends Ryan Reynolds (*Deadpool* and *Free Guy*) and Rob McElhenney (*It's Always Sunny in Philadelphia*).

Then another coworker told me about *Ted Lasso*.[32] *Ted Lasso* is full of puns, dad jokes, and relationships (good and bad). Lasso is an American team manager of a British football club (now you're starting to put the ramblings in this section together much like a bridge builder goes brick by brick).

Lasso initially stuck out like a sore thumb in the club because of his good-humored nature and kindness. He was a goldfish out of water. People didn't stop doing stupid things or being mean to him, but there was progress. His kindness created generosity in his circle, which we see clearly in the episodes about his panic attacks.

Lasso didn't try to manipulate anyone into having a friendship with him. He learned peoples' names because he wanted to know them. He brought his boss homemade cookies because it showed her that he cared about her. He believed he could make a positive impact, and he did all that he could to improve the lives of those around him—without any expectation that his kindness would be returned to him.

As far as I know, Lasso wasn't a Christian, but his attitude often reflected Christ. People saw that he was different, and it turned out they wanted more of it, and they were quite sad when he had to go. He repaired bridges that needed repair (often with a swift apology) and built bridges where there seemed to be no hope of reconciliation (hello, Jamie Tartt and Roy Kent). The show called it "The Lasso Effect."

We should have a similar influence as Christians—"The Christ Effect." It should be natural for us to want to repair relationships and build friendships with no ulterior motives other than living like Christ has called us to live. You're not earning your way to heaven by being nice to people. Instead, you're showing people what it's like to know Jesus, which should improve every aspect of your being, your character, and your world.

TRUTH + FRIENDSHIP = BRIDGE BUILDING

Bridge builders don't let subjective truths get in the way of relationships. In fact, different opinions amongst friends can increase the sustainability of the friendship, so long as respect is present. Indeed, it is refreshing in today's culture to step outside our echo chamber and connect with people who oppose our ideas. Doing that might even result in a better understanding of others and yourself. Psychologist Mark Travers put it this way: "By really listening to what others have to say and engaging in meaningful conversations with people who have different opinions, we can challenge our own biases and broaden our knowledge."[33] Think deeply about your friends and allow yourself to learn and grow and experience true life with them.

You're probably not going to have a deep relationship with someone the first time you meet them. You might not know much about them beyond where they work and what their family is like. Those basics are the building blocks of the foundation, and they are important. Each time you meet, you'll strengthen the foundation. You'll begin to trust them, and they'll begin to trust you.

Remember, your goal is not solely to share the gospel—you're sharing life with them, just like Jesus was willing to interact with people. Be a true friend others can rely upon. Be available so that when life is crumbling, you can be part of the support that helps them stand strong. You'll need the same from them. Bridge building is a two-way street. It is about making a way when there is no other way.

One note here: Do not elevate your desire for human friendship above your desire for disciple-making. We must be willing to make tough decisions if the Lord tells us to do so, even when it comes to relationships with others. Dietrich Bonhoeffer once wrote this warning about love, community, and friendship:

> Human love constructs its own image of the other person, of what he is and what he should become. It takes the life of the other person into its own hands. Spiritual love recognizes the true image of the other person which he has received from Jesus Christ, the image that Jesus Christ himself embodied and would stamp on all people.[34]

May we remember that human love is fleeting, and spiritual love is eternal. Keep that in mind as you pursue relationship with others, knowing that how you act and treat others directly reflects on Jesus' image within you.

BUILDING THE BRIDGE

Former US president Woodrow Wilson once said, "Friendship is the only cement that will ever hold the world together."[35] I think there's something to that, and it's one of the reasons why I so firmly believe friendship is foundational to bridge building. In a world that is often divided over such miniscule things as song lyrics and movie quotes and whatever social media tells us to be upset about, true friendship can break through the mess of it all. We can pick up the pieces when it feels like the world is falling apart around us. We can find common ground rather than stir division. Once we've let our guards down, we might even find that we're having fun being friendly. For some of us, doing this might be a change of pace because we've gotten so wrapped up in being alone. It's okay to admit that it might be nice to have a friend or two you trust—just look at what happened when Woody and Buzz Lightyear from *Toy Story* got over their differences and started seeing each other as potential friends. Their friendship changed the worlds of the other toys and even the humans around them.

Bridge building means taking a risk because being a kingdom builder isn't going to be easy. Jesus had friends, and He most assuredly laughed with them. He probably talked about things with His friends that never made it into Scripture. He loved them well and never compromised the truth, even when they challenged Him. May we be like Christ, willing to put ourselves out there for the sake of friendship, unity, shalom, and love. As bridge builders, we can have genuine friendships with people from other worldviews and cultures, and even with those who are hostile toward Christianity. That's what we'll cover in the next few chapters.

QUESTIONS FOR REFLECTION AND DISCUSSION

1. What does your circle of friends look like? Where can you find common ground, and where are you different?

2. Have you ever felt isolated and alone? How did you cope with those emotions?

3. How do friendships make you better, either generally or with a specific person in mind?

4. Have you ever had to pick up the pieces for a friend? If so, what did you learn from that experience?

5. What's a good way to speak truth to a friend, even if it is difficult to do so?

RECOMMENDED RESOURCES

Dale Carnegie, *How to Win Friends & Influence People* (New York: Pocket Books, 1998)

Charles E. Moore, *Called to Community: The Life Jesus Wants for His People* (Walden, NY: Plough Publishing, 2016)

Rebecca McLaughlin, *No Greater Love: A Biblical Vision for Friendship* (Chicago, IL: Moody, 2023)

INTERACTING WITH PEOPLE OF DIFFERENT WORLDVIEWS

If it is possible, as far as it depends on
you, live at peace with everyone.

ROMANS 12:18

If I say social media, what comes to your mind? Do you think (a) it is a great place where people can share their ideas in a safe environment, or (b) it is a place where people are belittled and demeaned if they dare state their beliefs publicly? I'm going to step out on a limb and say that you probably picked b. The same can be said of pretty much all social media, including YouTube.

I'll give you an example from earlier today (it's the reason I'm writing this section of the book at this very moment). I observed a thread on a social media platform in which the original poster (OP) called out what they thought was an incorrect worldview held by a specific person. Hundreds of comments later, all I saw were ad hominem attacks from all sides. Some were saying the OP shouldn't have posted what they believed, while others were pointing critical fingers at other commenters. Very few people were talking about the issue raised by the OP. Rather, they were discussing the people.

Friend, doing this will get you nowhere. The best I have seen from this thread is a few people graciously bowing out of the conversation and wishing the other folk well. Effective discourse rarely happens on social media. That's where good ideas go to die violent deaths at the hands of people who make assumptions about others or who have no time to consider thoughtful responses to their ideas.

Does that mean it's a waste of time to talk with others about important matters on social media? No. But I have found the best online conversations happen when all the parties involved approach others with the same respect they want. The Golden Rule—tweet unto others as you would have them tweet unto you, or something like that. I can't tell you the number of times I have seen non-Christians walk away from conversations online saying something like, "I am not surprised this is how Christians behave online. They are such hypocrites." Or, "You have just confirmed all of the bad things I thought about Christians. Thanks."

I recently read a poll conducted on social media by an atheist who asked others who was the most arrogant/hateful group to interact with online, and you know who won by a landslide? Evangelicals. It wasn't even close.[1] One person responded, "The Talibangelicals are the most abhorrent group of people in America."[2] Of course, not everyone thinks this way about Christians, but I think it's safe to say that we have a lot of work to do. We profess faith in Jesus and the transformation we've experienced because of Him, but our actions often say something different. This chapter will help you discuss your worldview with others in person and online without compromising the truth or your character.

KNOW YOUR OWN WORLDVIEW FIRST

In chapter 4, I discussed the decline of Bible reading in America. It's worse than simply not having good spiritual practices. Many of us don't truly know the worldview that we profess to believe. A worldview, in short, is your philosophy in life, the way you view the world. A more detailed answer is that a worldview is how you think about things like God, humanity, life, death, eternity, and purpose. Christianity would be considered a worldview.

In 2022, Lifeway Research released the results of their State of Theology survey, which focused on the worldview of Americans in general and professing American evangelicals.[3] Some of the more shocking findings include:

- 43 percent of professing evangelical respondents said that God changes, contrary to what Scripture says (see James 1:17 and Malachi 3:6).

- 56 percent of evangelical respondents said that all religions are acceptable to God, contrary to John 14:6.

- 43 percent of professing evangelical respondents said that Jesus was not God, just a great teacher, contrary to Romans 9:5.

- 38 percent (up from 13 percent in 2020) of evangelical respondents said religious belief is not objective truth.[4]

Some of these results are discouraging, especially when seen in context of previous years' results—things are not getting better. In chapter 8, I talked about how important it is to know truth and said that the Word of God is the best place to start. If we aren't opening our Bibles or going to church, how can we expect to understand or know what we believe? That won't happen magically. We can't just hope that we'll wake up with biblical knowledge; we've got to put in the work. This begins with reading our Bibles and being a part of a Christian community.

So, what is it that we believe? Here's a basic rundown of the Christian worldview.[5]

- **God**: immaterial, omnipotent (all-powerful), omnipresent (everywhere), omniscient (all-knowing), loving, just, infinite, holy, and the creator of everything

- **Jesus:** fully human, fully God, died on a cross, was physically resurrected three days after His death, ascended to heaven, the bridge between us and the Father, Savior of the world

- **Holy Spirit:** comforter, intercessor, powerful, truth, and advocate

- **Humanity:** made in God's image and likeness, sinful, and in need of a Savior

- **Salvation:** free gift through Christ's death and resurrection, works cannot save us, but they are a natural outpouring of our faith

- **Eternity:** heaven and hell exist

In a nutshell, Christianity states that humans were created by God, fell from grace (sin entered our story), found redemption and salvation in Christ, have an advocate in the Holy Spirit, and will experience eternity in some form or fashion. These beliefs come from Scripture, which is reliable, historical, and accurate.[6]

Notice that my list didn't include topics like baptism and women in leadership roles. I know I'm probably stepping in it by saying that, but bear with me. While those are certainly interesting issues to discuss amongst friends, they are not among the core beliefs of Christianity. We have to keep the main thing the main thing. The main thing—well, person—is Jesus.

Paul explains this well in Romans 14. The chapter is a warning to Christians passing judgment on fellow believers regarding secondary matters—in this case, food. They were fighting about which could be eaten and which could not. Clearly it was big enough of a problem that Paul heard about it. He admonished them (ever so gently) by reminding them that "the kingdom of God is not a matter of eating and drinking, but of righteousness, peace and joy in the Holy

Spirit, because anyone who serves Christ in this way is pleasing to God and receives human approval" (verses 17-18).

There are core issues, such as God's existence and the result of Jesus' resurrection. Then there are things that matter but are not salvific. That is, they play no part in your salvation. They might be interesting to discuss or debate, but they have no bearing on your identity as a Christian or your eternal future. Again, keep the main thing (main person, in our case) the main thing. As Christians, we have to know *why* we believe what we believe, but we have to know *what* we believe first. I encourage you to take the time to examine your worldview so that when asked by someone, you can boldly proclaim what it is you believe.

EXCLUSIVITY AND BRIDGE BUILDING

One complaint I hear frequently is that Christianity is not inclusive enough—we think we're the one, true way, and that makes us narrow-minded and intolerant toward other worldviews. To be fair, our faith rests on Christ who said, "I am the way and the truth and the life. No one comes to the Father except through me" (John 14:6). When compared with bumper-sticker theology statements like "Coexist" and other pluralistic mantras, what Jesus said certainly sounds exclusive. The truth is, it is. But Christianity, despite what the world may say, isn't the only religion that claims exclusivity. Muslims and Jewish people claim exclusivity, too, as do the adherents of Eastern religions, even those who seem to make it their business to show how inclusive they are.

Winfried Corduan, author of *Neighboring Faiths*, explained that although the Dalai Lama may have claimed in his Nobel Peace Prize speech that "all religions pursue the same goals," at another time he admitted he thought freedom was something "only Buddhists can accomplish."[7] Corduan reminds us that despite our ultimate desire to build bridges, "we cannot get away from the question of truth and falsehood. Not only do religions see themselves as the best and truest implicitly, but many religions, such as Christianity, Islam or Nichiren Shoshu, make explicit exclusivist claims."[8] His conclusion, which I agree with, is that logically, if one religion is true, the others must, therefore, be false.

Of course, as bridge builders, we can (and should) still glean truths from other worldviews. I'm not sure anyone gets it 100 percent wrong. As an example, New Agers often promote the sanctity of the earth. Now, they go too far by proclaiming the earth itself as a god. However, the fact that they consider creation care to be important is valid. We, too, as Christians, should take care of God's creation, including our planet. We shouldn't turn a blind eye to the damage humanity does to it, and we should try to prevent such damage. After all, the creation narrative in Genesis says, "The Lord God took the man and put him in the Garden of Eden to work it and take care of it" (2:15). Let's not forget this call.

Another example is Islam and piety. In general, Muslims value their worship of Allah, focusing on practices like fasting, prayer, and studying the Qur'an. Such piety should be present in the life of a Christian too. Our Savior was pious when He was here on earth, often retreating to communicate privately with His Father. Not only can we learn from Muslims in this way; we can find common ground with them by showing that we, too, value worshipping our God. Sometimes we spend so much time focusing on our differences that we fail to see the things that we can agree on.

CHARACTER COUNTS

The way people perceive or remember you is a reflection of your character. Do you leave them with a feeling of joy and peace, or of turmoil and destruction? Of course, you could leave them with no feeling at all, which would be better than something negative. Just as your behavior reflects your character, your character reflects your worldview. As a Christian, your character ought to reflect Jesus.

Apologist Amy Hall once said on a podcast, "Our character is representing Christ to other people. I think that's the biggest thing we have to keep in mind…When we respond to [people], character is a huge part. We want to represent Christ. We want to be truthful. We want to be humble. We want to show all the things that make Christ great so they can see who He is."[9] Our character speaks volumes about the truth we profess to proclaim.

DON'T MAKE ASSUMPTIONS

Let's face it. When it comes to other people, we make a lot of assumptions. We assume things about them based on their physical appearance and their body language, among other factors. We do the same when we hear someone holds certain worldviews. You might jump to conclusions about what they believe, why they believe it, and how their beliefs impact how they live. All without ever asking them personally what they believe. The problem is that your assumptions may very well be wrong. We saw earlier how many who profess to be Christians don't understand their own worldview; how can we assume to understand someone else's without hearing it from them directly? Bridge builders don't assume anything about anyone. Instead, they learn from others by asking questions and listening well.

ASK QUESTIONS, LISTEN WELL

I've touched on this tip throughout the book, and I believe it's at the core of what we do as bridge builders. To have firm foundations of both truth and friendship, we need to be able to ask questions and listen well.

In chapter 4, I touched on the importance of reading Scripture and how knowing the Word of God helps secure our foundation of truth. As Douglas Groothuis explained in *Christian Apologetics*:

> We must earnestly endeavor to know the truth of the biblical worldview and to make it known with integrity to as many people as possible with the best arguments available. To know God in Christ means that we desire to make truth available to others in the most compelling form possible.[10]

As we learned from John the Baptist, Thomas, and several other disciples, asking questions about truth can be transformative. If you're struggling to understand, ask for help. There's no shame in doing that, and in fact, it's nobler to ask rather than wallow in doubt. It's better for your heart and your mind.

Consider, for example, the situation with Philip and the Ethiopian man in Acts 8. Philip was instructed by an angel to travel on a certain road. As he did so, he saw a man reading in a chariot. The Spirit told Philip, "Go to that chariot and stay near it." Philip went up and asked the man, "Do you understand what you are reading?" (verses 26-30). The Ethiopian man was honest and said he needed help. Philip spent time explaining the Scripture passage to him, and (spoiler alert) the man was baptized as a result of Philip's time and effort (and surely with some help from the Holy Spirit). As Christians, we will encounter times of doubt. We should never be afraid to ask for help with what we do not understand about God, Jesus, the Bible, or anything else relating to our faith.

Another example is Lee Strobel, the author of *The Case for Christ*. He had ulterior motives when he started asking questions (he wanted his wife, Leslie, to stop being a Christian). Yet as he pursued truth, the experts he consulted were willing to take the time to help him sort through his questions. That led to Lee's conversion, and countless other lives have been changed as a result (including my husband Jay's). Asking questions when we wonder about things is excellent for building our foundation of truth.

Regarding the foundation of friendship, this one is a bit simpler because there's a common thread that unites humans, no matter our worldview or cultural background: We love to talk about ourselves because it makes us feel good.[11] Of course it feels good to be heard and valued because of our thoughts and feelings, but think about that for a minute. *It feels good to be heard.* We love to talk about ourselves when someone is listening to us. Shouldn't we then, knowing this, focus on listening well to others? The first step to listening well is asking good questions. Here are some questions to keep in mind when conversing with someone from a different worldview:

- How long have you been a [insert religion/worldview here], or how long have you believed [insert specific belief here]?

- Why do you believe your beliefs are true?

- What's the most interesting thing about your religion/belief system to you?

- What do your worship services look like? (Side note: If you are invited to attend, go!)

- Do you believe in prayer?

- What do you think about God, the universe, Jesus, etc.?

Once you've asked a question, *listen.* Don't start thinking about the next question you're going to ask. Really listen. In a 2011 TED Talk, Julian Treasure noted that we spend 60 percent of our time in conversations listening, but we retain only about 25 percent of what we hear.[12] Toward the end of his short lecture, Treasure recommended using the acronym RASA to listen better: Receive, Appreciate, Summarize, and Ask. That is, pay attention, engage with sounds of affirmation like "hmm," condense what you've heard, and ask follow-up questions.[13] Listening is such an essential skill in bridge building that we'll address it more in the next chapter as well as in chapter 14.

RELATED, BUT DIFFERENT

It can be tempting to try to bridge the gap between worldviews by highlighting our similarities at the expense of our differences—important differences, such as whether Jesus is God or the only way to heaven. Yes, New Agers and Christians both believe in creation care, but New Agers don't believe in the core Christian doctrine that Jesus died and was resurrected for their sins. They, instead, portend that Jesus was a man who was a great teacher.

All this to say, the gospel message is accessible to all people in all contexts. We must be willing to step into the fray, though. In his book *Neighboring Faiths*, Corduan concludes each chapter with "So you meet a [fill in the blank with the religion]" section. Part of his task here is to show how we can relate the gospel to anyone from any worldview. Corduan reminds us to avoid using Hindu terms to relate to Christianity and notes that the gospel has been relatively simple to share through Christian missions in places like India because the Hindu people have seen examples of love and sacrifice.[14] Interestingly, Corduan suggests that for some worldviews, seeds of doubt—or as Greg Koukl calls them, "pebbles in shoes"[15]—work best when sharing the gospel.[16] The takeaway? Every person is unique, and the process of bridge building is not a cookie-cutter situation. This is why it's so important for bridge builders to listen well to others, particularly when learning about their worldview.

DON'T GO IN WITH GUNS BLAZING

I don't know about you, but when I learn something new, I get excited about sharing that something with someone else. For instance, a friend of mine recently took me on a ride in her new car. She taught me all about the different functions on the car, including features like self-driving and how few seconds it took to get up to 70 miles per hour. When I got home later that day, I rambled on and on to my husband about how cool her car was and how I want one someday. He told me he'd never heard me get so ramped up about a car before, and I realized that it was because my friend was enthusiastically sharing with me about her car, which caused me to receive enthusiastically. Then all I wanted to do was share that enthusiasm.

I'm not telling you to curb your enthusiasm about worldview or Christianity. I'm just asking you to take a step back and consider the effects. Remember the scene in *Nacho Libre* where Nacho crudely and forcibly baptizes Esquelito before a wrestling match? That's not what we're going for with bridge building. Yes, be excited about your faith. Be thrilled by what God has done for you through Jesus. But do not attempt to "baptize" your friends without their permission because you are concerned about their salvation. Be concerned, not forceful.

ALLOW OTHERS TO SHARE WITH YOU

I had a friend who was a Latter-day Saint (commonly known as Mormon) in college invite me to her ward and give me my first Book of Mormon. She wrote a beautiful note in it, and it sits on a shelf with the other copies I've collected over the years. Shortly after, I read it from cover to cover. I also visited her ward with her (the service was more than three hours long back then!).

I learned a lot about my friend's beliefs during that time, and knowing her has helped me as I've interacted with other Latter-day Saints since then. One of my favorite recent podcast conversations was with a young woman named Mariah.[17] She was trying to figure out what she believed, and during that time, two Latter-day Saint missionaries knocked on her door. She had started attending a ward but still had questions about her newfound faith. I had an hour-long exchange with her about some of her beliefs. We bonded (naturally) over things like our sorority memberships, but my biggest takeaway was how easily the dialogue flowed, even when discussing the views of her religion. We both listened to one another, and neither of us asked the other questions that were antagonistic or ugly. Our intent was to learn from one another, and I think we both walked away from that podcast better humans because of our chat.

So, when missionaries come to your door, don't immediately turn them away. Instead, take some time out of your day and learn about what they believe. You may learn something you didn't know before. You may develop more empathy. You may even realize that it's enjoyable to talk about different faiths with others. And it may result in an opportunity for you to share your own faith.

BE HUMBLE

Gear up, because I'm about to rip off a Band-Aid: You're wrong about something. It might be how you pronounce a particular place. Or maybe you mess up the lyrics of your favorite song and don't even realize it. Or maybe something in your theology is amiss (e.g., egalitarian/complementarian, baptism, getting tattoos, etc.). Like I explained in chapter 3, bridge builders will admit when they are wrong. They are humble and are willing to learn. Humility is an outpouring of love for another; indeed, those who are humble will be exalted by the Lord Himself (Matthew 23:12).

Consider the prodigal son Jesus describes in Luke 15. The son takes his inheritance and squanders it. In shame he returns home, and his father is happy to see him—so much so that he throws a party in his son's honor. The son learned a couple of valuable lessons: (1) sleeping with pigs is gross, and (2) forgiveness is possible with humility and a desire to grow. If he hadn't been willing to admit his wrongdoing and ask for his father's forgiveness, he probably would not have left the pigpen.

Bridge building requires humility. You should be able to admit it when you're wrong. You should also be able to see all the ways others get it right. Someone must be wrong in the baptism debate (infant baptism or not). Someone must be wrong in the egalitarian/complementarian debate (women preachers or not). Someone must be wrong about tattoos. Someone must be wrong about a lot of issues, and *it might be you.*

WHAT'S FOR DINNER?

When I was a missionary kid, we lived in a third-world country. One of the rules was that we were supposed to eat any food that was offered to us—it was rude to refuse. So we did. There was a time when we were offered fish soup, and, well, it contained the entire fish, eyes and all. My mom once told me about finding a whole horse head for sale at a market in Guatemala. Sometimes we didn't know what we were eating. By taking what we were offered, we were accepting hospitality. In essence, we were transcending cultural boundaries and keeping up with social norms.

An easy way to build a bridge to your neighbors is to invite them over for dinner. If you know that your neighbors practice a different religion or are from another culture, it would be kind to ask if they have dietary restrictions. That's a simple way to build a bridge, and it is very unlikely that anyone would be offended by your inquiry. In fact, I'd recommend asking everyone you invite into your home if they have dietary issues you need to be aware of. Otherwise, you might not find out until it's too late, and that magnificent meal goes to waste. And if you go over to someone else's home, be gracious and grateful for whatever it is you are served. Adopt a missionary mindset, even if what you're offered isn't what you expected or wanted. You might very well discover you have a new favorite meal and one more thing in common with your neighbor.

PLANT SEEDS, NOT WEEDS

When I was in seminary, I was talking with a friend about conversations with people from different worldviews, and he said, "We need to plant seeds, not weeds." For anyone who has ever tried to maintain a garden (or even just a front yard), you know how weeds can destroy. The same is true about our words. Just think of the last time someone said something mean or rude to you. Despite the childhood mantra "Sticks and stones may break my bones, but words will never hurt me," words can cause significant damage. I know that I'm still affected by harsh words I received from classmates as a child. You can't just uproot them and expect them to stay away forever. Weeds are persistent little buggers, and the weedy words we allow to spread can cause harm for years to come.

Friend, if you engage in gossip, please stop. Gossip is the type of weed that is nearly impossible to remove once it's taken root. Scripture is very clear about gossip and its weedy nature:

- "Do not let any unwholesome talk come out of your mouths, but only what is helpful for building others up according to their needs, that it may benefit those who listen" (Ephesians 4:29).

- "Without wood a fire goes out; without gossip a quarrel dies down" (Proverbs 26:20).

- "Those who consider themselves religious and yet do not

keep a tight rein on their tongues deceive themselves, and their religion is worthless" (James 1:26).

If someone comes to you in confidence, keep their confidence. Don't spread the word. Gossip not only betrays trust, but it also destroys bridges. Gossip is an unyielding crack that will ruin the foundations of truth and friendship and level the bridge. You may not get a chance to start over, and you may impede the seeds others have planted along the way.

In your conversations, you should also avoid ad hominem attacks. An ad hominem (Latin for "aimed at the man") attack is when a person stops addressing the topic at hand and instead, makes a personal, disparaging remark. For example, imagine you're having a discussion with a friend about Jesus. Then, all of a sudden, that person says you're dumb. That's an ad hominem attack. It adds nothing to the value of the debate and distracts from the issue you were talking about in the first place.

Keep in mind, too, that it's not just words that are weedy. Your actions can do a lot of damage too. Even a negative look (intentional or not) can plant a weed. Be mindful of how you present yourself to others, understanding that people are watching and have certain expectations because of who you profess to be. If you claim to be a Christian, act like a Christ follower. Yield good fruit. Don't kill it.

BUILDING THE BRIDGE

The first step to engaging well with others who have different beliefs than you is to know your own worldview. Once you've got a firm grasp on what you believe and why you believe it's true, you can participate well in a conversation with another person about faith. Don't assume anything about what they do or do not believe, and don't resort to personal insults; instead, ask questions, listen well, and follow their lead as far as which direction the conversation goes. Maintain a Christlike attitude throughout your engagement and recognize that you are planting seeds (don't plant weeds). Bridge building is a team sport. Sometimes you'll share about yourself, and other times, they will share about themselves.

QUESTIONS FOR REFLECTION AND DISCUSSION

1. Which worldviews are represented in your circle of friends?

2. Have you ever accidentally burned a bridge to someone because you went in with guns blazing? How might you repair that relationship (recognizing that sometimes repair isn't always possible)?

3. Have you ever invited anyone from a different religion over for dinner? If so, what considerations were made for their beliefs (e.g., dietary restrictions)?

4. Think about a time when you had to admit you were wrong (or should have admitted it). How did you handle the situation, and was there anything you would have done differently?

5. What are some ways you can plant seeds in your circle?

RECOMMENDED RESOURCES

Matt Brown, *Truth Plus Love: The Jesus Way to Influence* (Grand Rapids, MI: Zondervan, 2019)

Paul Copan, *When God Goes to Starbucks: A Guide to Everyday Apologetics* (Ada, MI: Baker Books, 2008)

Finding Something Real podcast featuring Janell Wood

Win Corduan, *Neighboring Faiths: A Christian Introduction to World Religions*, 3d ed. (Downers Grove, IL: InterVarsity Press, 2024)

Daniel McCoy, ed., *The Popular Handbook of World Religions* (Eugene, OR: Harvest House, 2021)

NAVIGATING CULTURAL DIVIDES

We build too many walls and not enough bridges.

ISAAC NEWTON

MAGA. BLM. LGBTQ+. Isn't it interesting how acronyms carry so much weight? What are your thoughts when you see someone with a MAGA sticker on their truck or a BLM sign in their front yard? What if they have a rainbow in their social media profile? These letters and symbols either elicit warm fuzzies inside you or incite feelings of anger or pain. Just look at a typical US presidential election year.

In 2015, our family moved to Montgomery, Alabama, for the summer. We wanted to be a part of the community, so we enrolled our daughter in gymnastics at a local gym, frequented local shops and restaurants, and immersed ourselves in the historical downtown area. I will never forget the day that the governor of Alabama ordered the removal of the Confederate flag from the capitol. One day, it flew high, and the next, it was gone. It was a historical moment in Alabama's history, one that I was glad our daughter was able to see. This isn't a book about politics or particular beliefs, but it *is* a book that will address some elephants in the room. The Confederate battle flag (the one taken down at the capitol in Alabama on June 24,

2015) is a symbol. You might see it one way, and your neighbor may see it another. And that's the point I'm trying to make. How will you know if you don't ask? Racial division isn't uncommon in our world—it is not limited to the United States. I first understood the worldwide tension in 1999.

When I was a senior in high school, I attended the Future World Leaders Summit through A Presidential Classroom, a program for students throughout the world (half from the US, half from other countries). At the summit we had a mock UN, visited our nation's most historical sites, and focused on international relations. I made a few lifelong friends that week. The highlight, though, was seeing a relationship form between an Israeli student and a Palestinian student. These young people came from across the world and were assigned to the same group. They entered the week with preconceived negative notions about one another, and they left as friends.

At our closing ceremony, the Israeli and Palestinian students spoke of a renewed hope that perhaps they could bridge a way forward for their people and peace in their part of the world. History tells us that tensions escalated in 2000, and they remain high between the two people groups even today. But for that week, those young men saw an opportunity for shalom in their region. This is what Jesus was trying to do with the Jewish people and the Samaritans. In fact, as Rebecca McLaughlin notes in her award-winning book *Confronting Christianity*, "Jesus scandalized His fellow Jews by tearing through racial and cultural boundaries."[1] He was a so-called troublemaker but carried out His mission with grace, mercy, and a whole lot of love.

SAMARITANS AND JEWISH PEOPLE

Perhaps the best example of cultural schisms in Scripture (though there are many we can learn from) is that between the Samaritans and the Jews. Samaritans were considered less-than by the Jewish people because they were a mixed race. Despite their physical proximity to each other (separated by about 30 miles), they might as well have been worlds apart. They hated each other. The political and cultural rift between the two groups had existed for about 1,000 years. Not surprisingly, Jesus came to change all that.

Scripture gives us glimpses of Jesus' work in that direction, and we see it most clearly in His parable of the good Samaritan (Luke 10:25-37). Here, we find direct interaction with a Jewish person who likely had many negative thoughts about Samaritans, thoughts that had been engrained probably since birth. An expert in Torah law asked Jesus how to inherit eternal life. Jesus asked the lawyer what the law said. The expert replied with a reference to Deuteronomy 6:5 and Leviticus 19:18: "'Love the Lord your God with all your heart and with all your soul and with all your strength and with all your mind'; and, 'Love your neighbor as yourself'" (verse 27). Jesus affirmed the lawyer's answer and said, "Do this and you will live" (verse 28). The conversation could have ended there, but the expert pushed Jesus further. He asked for clarification about neighbors—who exactly counts as a neighbor? That's when Jesus replied with the story of the good Samaritan.

The surprising part was that the hero in this parable, which was told to a Jewish person, happened to be a Samaritan. The Samaritan stumbled upon a man who had been robbed. The man was not helped by a priest or even a Levite (an assistant to a priest). No, he was saved by a Samaritan. The lesson? Everyone is your neighbor, even the ones with whom you have conflict.

Now before you begin to think that Jesus didn't understand the clash between the Samaritans and Jews, recall that He had already been rejected by the Samaritans in Luke 9. Jesus and His disciples were on their way to Jerusalem, and He had sent them ahead to find a place to stay during their travels. The people in a Samaritan village refused to allow them to stay there (verses 52-53). You see, the

Samaritans worshipped the Lord at Mount Gerizim[2] (they continue this practice even today!), while the Jewish people traditionally worshipped at the temple in Jerusalem. Most Jewish people traveling to Jerusalem would simply walk around the Samaritan village to avoid it, even though that meant many extra miles of travel. Jesus didn't want to do that despite the traditional hostility that existed between the two people groups.

Interestingly, James and John got quite upset at the Samaritans' rejection—so much so that they asked Jesus if they should "call fire down from heaven to destroy them" (verse 54). Jesus rebuked them for their suggestion. He simply respected the Samaritans' wishes and went through a different village on the way to Jerusalem.

So, Jesus understood the tension, and yet He encouraged His disciples to think and act differently about their so-called enemies. Everyone is our neighbor—we don't get to choose who we extend grace and mercy to. We are called to be like the good Samaritan in Luke 10. To love our neighbors, we need to be willing to interact with them.

THE OTHER SIDE OF THE TRACKS

The US has a difficult history when it comes to seeing people who aren't like us. The phrase "the other side of the tracks" has become an expression of our differences—people on one side are kept away by a barrier, in this case, iron rods. Often, the tracks separate white neighborhoods from Black ones. In fact, the phrase may have a history related to economic status—the sootier side of the tracks (where the soot was directed by the wind as the train traveled through town) was where the undesirables lived. The phrase has lost its impact these days, but one need only look at our world to see that such divisions remain.

From slavery to inequity in our justice system to racial divides that exist even today, Christians find themselves at a crossroads, and we have an opportunity to be the bridge to *shalom* (wholeness). Our family recently rewatched the film *Remember the Titans*. The film is roughly based on a true story of a Virginian high school football team in the early 1970s. Although *Brown v. Board of Education* (347 U.S. 483 [1954]) had long since established that racial segregation in public schools was outlawed, it was a slow burn. Schools had willfully rejected the mandate. That was the setting when a Black man became the head coach of a newly integrated football team. The town was divided. The team was divided. Even the coaching staff was divided. And yet, the players and coaching staff persisted and dominated in their region that season.

The reality is that we are *all* from the other side of the tracks. The film touches on the heart of what it means to show love to others—civility, courage, and compassion. Another illustration of these characteristics is the relationship between Ruby Bridges and her teacher, Barbara Henry.

BUILDING BRIDGES WITH RUBY

Ruby Bridges's story began before she was born, when her future teacher, Barbara Henry, was being raised in Boston in the 1930s and 1940s. It was then that Henry "learned to appreciate and enjoy our important commonalities, amid our external differences of class, community, or color."[3] Henry began her teaching career overseas, then returned to the US and moved to New Orleans with her family. In 1960, a six-year-old Black girl would change her life.

Integration was new in the area, and as schools were being desegregated, white families were removing their children. Henry was the only teacher at William Frantz Elementary School willing to teach Ruby, who had to be escorted into the school by four armed US federal marshals. If you've never seen the image of Ruby on the steps of her new school, you should look it up. It's incredible to think that the

mere presence of a small six-year-old girl would incite riots and protests—protests where she was once welcomed to school "by a woman
displaying a black doll in a wooden coffin."[4] It was a moment when
Ruby needed hope, and Henry filled that gap. In an interview with
Oprah in 1996, when Henry was asked if having Ruby as a student
was difficult, she said:

> Well, it was wonderful to have a little student like Ruby
> that it really made it a pleasure. It was a sad time indeed,
> and it was an anxious time…I assumed I would be teaching
> a class, and so we had a grand time together, I think, side
> by side, just the two of us. We spent the year together.[5]

It was an understatement, I think, to say that it was a sad time. Every
other student was pulled from Henry's class, and Ruby could not eat
in the cafeteria or go to recess. Bathroom breaks required an escort
by a federal marshal. In due course, it got easier, but that first year
wouldn't have happened if Henry hadn't stood in the gap. Ruby later
said, "Mrs. Henry was the nicest teacher I ever had. She tried very
hard to keep my mind off what was going on outside."[6] Henry built
a bridge with the community with her courage, and eventually, the
rest of the world moved on and all the kids came back to school.

If we look in history, and even in modernity, we see instances
of people building bridges with others like Henry did with Ruby.
Bridge builders are willing to take risks, even at the cost of their lives.
Jesus' disciples understood this when they continued to lead the early
church after their Lord's ascension into heaven. According to tradition,
Paul, our favorite gospel-centric bridge builder, was beheaded. I'm
not saying that you need to go and martyr yourself to prove you're a
bridge builder, but being willing to speak up in a culture when perhaps we aren't encouraged to do so can say so much to the people
you're standing in the gap for. These days, unfortunately, something

that looks like speaking against culture is actually getting in the way of bridge building—the cancel culture.

YOU'RE CANCELED

The fact of the matter is that our world isn't divided only by racial issues. That's but one point of conflict among many. To cancel someone—typically a celebrity or a business—is to boycott or blacklist them due to words or actions often related to politics or social issues. This phenomenon has been going on for some years, and people on all sides are getting in on the action.[7] Consider these examples from recent years:

- In 2017, Dove was accused of racism when it aired an ad featuring a Black woman morphing into a white woman (the ad was about soap and getting clean).

- In 2023, Bud Light took a major hit (socially and financially) when it promoted trans influencer Dylan Mulvaney. That same year, Target was canceled due to its decision to sell trans-friendly swimsuits in the children's section of their stores.

- Both Hobby Lobby and Chick-fil-A have been canceled due to their leaders' views regarding homosexuality.

- Singer Kanye West was briefly canceled after he took to the stage to say Beyonce was robbed when Taylor Swift won the 2009 MTV Best Female Video award. He's since been canceled for other reasons, from bizarre behavior to shirts he wears to basketball games.

- Actor Jonah Hill was canceled in 2023 when a series of texts

between him and his girlfriend were made public, which
led to him being labeled a sexist misogynist.

- Singer Jason Aldean was canceled in 2023 when he released
a song called "Try That in a Small Town," a song that ref-
erenced guns and promoted the Second Amendment right
to bear arms.

Of course, cancel culture is grounded in consumerism—we can
spend our money where we want to and choose to withdraw our
financial support when something upsets us. It's the American way.
However, cancel culture has become more aggressive and toxic, and
many have warned against its purpose. In fact, it can make us forget
what we're fighting for in the first place. For example, regardless of
what we might think of the teachings of Pope Francis of the Catho-
lic Church, he made this astute observation:

> Under the guise of defending diversity, *it ends up cancelling
> all sense of identity, with the risk of silencing positions that
> defend a respectful and balanced understanding of various
> sensibilities.* A kind of dangerous "one-track thinking"
> [pensée unique] is taking shape, one constrained to deny
> history or, worse yet, to rewrite it in terms of present-
> day categories, whereas any historical situation must be
> interpreted in the light of a hermeneutics of that particular
> time, not that of today[8] (emphasis added).

A number of prominent people have lamented about society's ten-
dency to cancel or call out what or whom we disagree with. We all
have this potential—to lament something we do ourselves. We know
it's wrong, and yet when it benefits us, we participate. Unfortunately,
cancel culture fails to see the big picture. Humans are caught up in
waves of emotion, and the decision to cancel is often rooted in anger.

Sometimes our anger is valid. Sometimes it's righteous. Sometimes, it merits swift action, and in our world, that typically means cancellation or boycott. But as bridge builders, we need to think about the impact of our decisions. Cancelling a product or brand often results in huge losses for the people who work for said companies—the little people, if you will. We shouldn't take such action without considering the impact. Indeed, boycotts are typically short-lived.[9] People are fickle. The same people up in arms about Target one week are back in those stores the next. Viewers cancel Netflix, but then Netflix streams a show they love, so they return a month or two later.

Perhaps this is why the Bible warns us to "set [our] minds on things above, not on earthly things" (Colossians 3:2) and reminds us that "the mind governed by the flesh is death, but the mind governed by the Spirit is life and peace" (Romans 8:6). Let's not be known by who or what we cancel; instead, let's be known as peacemakers who yearn to understand and show compassion toward others, even when we disagree.

POLITICS AND DISUNITY

If I say, "US presidential elections," what is your immediate feeling? I have to be honest with you: It makes me feel icky. It's not so much the outcome that makes me feel that way, but the process that got us there. I used to enjoy politics, or at least I did in theory. I enjoyed debates and the ritual of going to the voting booth and casting my ballot.

It wasn't an election that ruined politics for me. The turning point for me was the confirmation hearing for US Supreme Court chief justice John Roberts, who was nominated by former US president George W. Bush in 2005. That was the first time I saw the deep chasm that exists between Democrats and Republicans. Speaking about the nomination process in general, the chief justice said that "the votes were, I think, strictly on party lines for the last three of them, or close to it, and that doesn't make any sense. That suggests to me that the process is being used for something other than ensuring the qualifications of the nominees."[10] His own confirmation was indicative of the split—not a single Republican voted against his confirmation, and the Democrats were divided down the middle.[11]

This matters because it hasn't always been that way. The president generally used to find a qualified candidate, and that person was typically easily confirmed. Now, that's no longer the way it works. In fact, I'd venture to say that the ability to nominate justices for the US Supreme Court is now a major issue on the presidential ballot. The process has been politicized. And yet, the Supreme Court has traditionally been neutral. During the State of the Union address, the justices remain seated (despite the congressional members standing and clapping for what seems like forever, or booing if they are from the other political party).

But what does the US Supreme Court have to do with bridge building? Well, I think the current state of Supreme Court confirmation hearings is an indication that not all is well in US politics. Things have gotten so bad, in fact, that two out of five Americans think it's likely we'll have another civil war sometime in the next decade.[12] Not only that, 66 percent of Americans think things have gotten worse since 2021, and 62 percent expect political divisions to continue to increase.[13] It does seem like people are becoming more divided with each successive national election.

There's hope, though, friend. There are organizations like the Millennial Action Project that are trying to build bridges in our democracy.[14] At the heart of the potential solutions for our current state is peaceful discussions between parties. We've seen this work before—bipartisanship isn't dead, it's just dormant. And we can be the change we wish to see.

In Patrick Schreiner's book *Political Gospel*, we're reminded that our purpose is not to promote any earthly kingdom. "Our primary political message," he says, "should press our people to stay loyal to King Jesus."[15] He continues:

> Since government is a common good, we should be the first in line to seek the good of the city. This means being active citizens, pressing toward and praying for the flourishing of our communities and nation…faithful citizenship is a Christian mandate.[16]

Instead of getting wrapped up in angry politics,[17] let's get focused on our mission: to be bridge builders who plant seeds so that Jesus will be known as Savior of the world. Start looking past politics and seeing the people behind the issues.

COMPASSION IS FOR PEOPLE YOU SEE

It is hard to show compassion to people you can't (won't) see—the priest and Levite in the parable of the good Samaritan didn't even see someone like them. But the Samaritan saw his so-called enemy and showed him mercy. There's another example of this type of care in Mark 8. Jesus was gathered with a crowd of 4,000 non-Jewish men, plus women and children. They had been together for three days, and Jesus realized they were hungry for literal food, not simply spiritual food. Jesus understood that they were physically hungry because He was hungry; He was, after all, fully human. He fed all of them with just seven loaves of bread and a few fish.

One of the key aspects of this narrative is that Jesus showed the people compassion. He knew that they had traveled from far distances, and He was concerned that if He let them leave hungry, they might not make it home. Jesus was compassionate, and He was teaching His disciples to be compassionate, too, by extending a helping hand to Gentiles. This would have been unusual because it was a non-Jewish crowd (contrast this with the feeding of 5,000 in Mark 6), and Jesus was showing His followers that they needed to see "others." We cannot extend compassion if we do not see.

How often do we miss others because we simply do not see them? Jesus was certainly building a bridge in His feeding miracle. He ensured that all of His people, even the Gentiles, were both spiritually and physically fed. Bridge building requires us to see people as God sees them—as image bearers He loves deeply. We should also extend such love and compassion. Sometimes bridge building means we step outside of our comfort zone and get to know people outside of our typical community because God's community is full of all types of people He loves and cares for. Perhaps that's what Jesus meant when He told His disciples, "Open your eyes and look at the fields! They are ripe for harvest" (John 4:35). We can't impact the world if we can't even see it. Let's open our eyes.

HOPE ON THE HORIZON

An initiative called Bridging Differences, which is spearheaded by the organization Greater Good Science Center, aims to promote "the skills and social conditions that are critical to reducing polarization and promoting more constructive dialogue."[18] The center is not a Christian organization, and it may suggest things that would not align with the Christian worldview; however, its efforts to help others build bridges is commendable and presents a model that Christians can follow as we engage in bridge building. The Bridging Differences initiative offers a variety of resources toward that end. There are other resources online that encourage people to set aside their differences and unite for the common good. The reality is that we are not always going to agree on everything. But we can have more constructive conversations that yield better fruit. The leaders of the

Bridging Differences initiative, Scott Shigeoka and Jason Marsh, note that some bridges require more work than others.

> While crossing a long bridge is an ambitious and worthwhile goal, we shouldn't underestimate the significance, and even the challenges, of crossing some smaller bridges, as well. Indeed, crossing those short bridges can be good practice for ultimately crossing the longer ones.[19]

In other words, we shouldn't shy away from bridges just because they seem too easy or, on the flip side, too daunting. This is especially true for Christians, who should prioritize perseverance. Take it one brick at a time, recognizing that nothing may come of it. You may walk away with an unfinished bridge. That doesn't mean your effort was wasted. Remember, you're planting seeds, not weeds. Making the effort may not change another person, but it could change you. The reality is, as Rebecca McLaughlin notes in *Confronting Christianity*, history indicates that Christianity "is the most diverse, multiethnic, and multicultural movement in all of history."[20] We'd be remiss to forget our past, and we'd be sorely wrong if we forgot who we were made to be in Christ—ours is a worldview that loves all people because we understand they are called to be children of God.

BE THE CHANGE

I was a pretty big Michael Jackson fan growing up. I didn't know a lot about his personal life; I just loved his music. His song "Man in the Mirror" has always been my favorite because it talks about our responsibility to see the need and make the change, not waiting for someone else to do it. One simple way bridge builders can make changes despite cultural differences is to open up the lines of communication. Keep in mind, too, that you do not need to agree on everything to have a fruitful friendship. Friends disagree sometimes. Friends even fight sometimes.

I'll give you an example from my own life. I once said something really stupid (okay, I have done plenty of dumb things in my lifetime, but I'm talking about a more recent experience). I messed up, and I needed to apologize, but my friend was angry (and understandably so), so she needed some distance. The next day, we talked, and recently, she told me we were better for the experiences we've had, the good and the bad. I agree. Now, I wish I hadn't been dumb, but we do dumb things. We do not mean to mess up, but we're human. We're most likely not trying to make people upset. But when we do, we should apologize and sometimes we have to wait—wait well and pray for the best. The person may accept your apology, or they may not. Be willing to accept either outcome and stay humble and meek.

BUILDING THE BRIDGE

I admit that I'm not a fan of watching the news because I don't want to hear about someone else being canceled or the latest political shenanigans. My recommendation to you? Go on a media fast, and I am almost 100 percent sure you'll be better for it in the end. Doom scrolling is dimming the light in your world.[21] Turn off the news and see the light beyond the screen. It can be healing, and it may even allow you to see people and to be more open to understanding the people you currently wouldn't normally reach out to. Get off the computer and get into conversations with them. Find out where you have common ground and begin to build a relationship based on what is similar. Perhaps you'll find that you're not as different as you once thought.[22]

QUESTIONS FOR REFLECTION AND DISCUSSION

1. Reflecting on my story about the fish soup, when have you done something out of respect to participate in a cultural norm?

2. When have you let cultural issues keep you from building bridges?

3. In what ways could you benefit from a media fast? If you've done a media fast, what happened?

4. In what ways can you be humbler or more forgiving in your interactions with others?

5. Are there any changes you can make in your own life that can help build bridges despite culture issues?

RECOMMENDED RESOURCES

Brandon Washington, *A Burning House: Redeeming American Evangelicalism by Examining Its History, Mission, and Message* (Grand Rapids, MI: Zondervan, 2023)

Eric Mason, *Urban Apologetics: Cults and Cultural Ideologies: Biblical and Theological Challenges Facing Christians* (Grand Rapids, MI: Zondervan, 2023)

Patrick Schreiner, *Political Gospel: Public Witness in a Politically Crazy World* (Nashville: B&H Publishing, 2022)

Rebecca McLaughlin, *Confronting Christianity: 12 Hardest Questions for the World's Largest Religion* (Wheaton, IL: Crossway, 2019)

Joe Dallas, *Christians in a Cancel Culture: Speaking with Truth and Grace in a Hostile World* (Eugene, OR: Harvest House, 2021)

RESPONDING TO THOSE WHO MAKE FUN OF CHRISTIANITY AND THE BIBLE

...love has within it a redemptive power. And there is a power there that eventually transforms individuals.

MARTIN LUTHER KING JR.[1]

I don't know about you, but some comedy makes me uncomfortable, especially the kind that uses disparaging remarks to drive home the punch line. We see this a lot at televised awards shows, and stand-up comedians often take jabs at audience members for a laugh. Apparently (and unfortunately), such humor is on the rise,[2] and Christians aren't immune from it.

For example, there's a video of comedian David Cross (you might know him from *Arrested Development* or *Alvin and the Chipmunks*) in which he is criticizing the Bible and Christians who believe it's true. During his act, he says that the Bible is a copy of a copy that has been translated and retranslated. He calls the Bible "the world's oldest game of telephone."[3] What strikes me most about the video isn't the punch line—no, what strikes me most is the laughter. He has the crowd rolling because they think it is such a funny joke.

And it is hard not to take it personally because I believe the Bible is true and not at all like the game of telephone. The Bible wasn't a secret shared from one person to the next—it was copied meticulously by people who cared about being accurate. Did some mistakes happen in the process of copying the text? Yes, but minimally and nothing that affects the key teachings of Scripture.[4] Yet the audience laughed because perhaps they believed the lie that the Bible isn't reliable.

For some people, it is easy to make fun of others for any number of so-called strange beliefs. Christianity falls into that category for many, and as a result, many a joke has been told at the Christian's expense. Don't believe me? Think about how Christians are often portrayed in television shows or in films. They are frequently shown as hypocritical and judgmental—Flanders on *The Simpsons*, or the warden in *Shawshank Redemption*.[5] There are exceptions, of course (the Taylors on *Friday Night Lights* or Blanche in *New in Town*), but extremes sell in Hollywood, so the exceptions are few and far between.

Maybe you've experienced ridicule because of your faith. I know that I have, and not just on X. In law school, I was labeled extreme by someone because I supported a particular political candidate. My fellow classmate had no qualms about talking meanly about my faith behind my back.

So how can we respond when this happens? It would be easy to get offended, take it personally, and react emotionally, but those aren't the best way to build bridges. Instead, we should respond the way Christ did to His accusers—with love. This chapter will help you with some practical tips on how to respond like Jesus when we're faced with mockery and taunts.

DON'T TAKE IT PERSONALLY

For the most part, I have had kind responses to my faith from people who know me personally. Even in law school, I had an atheist friend who told me she could trust me because she knew I followed Jesus. It was no secret I was a Christian—I kept a Bible at my desk, and I read it regularly between classes (that, my friend, is how you survive law school unscathed!). I've had other atheist friends ask very good questions about my beliefs, but with respect, not cruelty. The most awful remarks I have heard from nonbelievers have come from online interactions. I understand how hard it can be to endure mean comments and quick jabs from non-Christians. It would be easy to leave social media in the dust, but then I'd leave friends I've made and the potential for healthy and loving conversations.

One thing that has helped me endure is recognizing that most of the time, it is not about me. If others are criticizing your looks, you should reject those comments immediately and remind yourself you are made in the image of God. If they are criticizing something you've said, examine your words and determine whether you need to retract them and apologize or let them stand. If, however, they are mocking Jesus or God or anything found in Scripture, it's not about you. Even if they are mocking the church or its people, it is probably not about you.

Those who are hostile toward Christianity usually have had previous bad experiences with Christians that cause them to express ill-will toward all Christians (but don't assume that is why—every person's experience is different). That's not difficult to understand, though. Many of us have had bad experiences in church or at the hands of other Christians. Author Reba Riley calls the current religious landscape "Post-Traumatic Church Syndrome."[6] And she hits the nail on the head as to why we need to see people as beloved the way Jesus saw them—losing your religion can impact your entire life.

> People who leave or are left by their faith lose a lot more than a place to go on Sunday morning. They lose relationships with family and friends, social status, tribal approval, self-esteem. They lose their God, their identity, their certainty, their gravity. I know because I lost all those things.[7]

And losing everything is painful and tragic and worth approaching with love. If we choose to respond when someone mocks us, we should do so with empathy and care—"be kind and compassionate to one another" (Ephesians 4:32). Show the same compassion Jesus did to the woman at the well or any of the people He healed throughout His ministry. Saying something as simple as "I'm sorry that happened to you" with genuine care can be life changing. True kindness can chip away at the hard exterior wall that has been built up and begin to build a bridge to healing.

DEFEND THE GOSPEL, NOT YOURSELF

I don't know about you, but when I'm in an argument, I'm quick to defend myself. Maybe it is because I'm trained in the law that it seems to come so naturally that I want to prove why I'm right. Of course, Scripture tells us to do the exact opposite of that: "My dear brothers and sisters, take note of this: Everyone should be quick to listen, slow to speak and slow to become angry, because human anger does not produce the righteousness that God desires" (James 1:19-20). To be sure, the situation is different when you're defending the gospel (1 Peter 3:15), but if you're only defending yourself, take a step back, breathe deeply, and slow down.

Easier said than done, right? When someone accuses you of something or even if they are merely suggesting that you fold the towels a different way or organize your office differently, you're probably more likely to defend yourself, telling them all the ways that you are right, and they are wrong. You want to be heard, you want to be understood, and you want to be accepted. Speaking "your truth" has become the norm. Humanity isn't naturally slow to speak and quick to listen, are we? Especially in the age of social media.

We get more likes/shares the more quickly we respond, especially if our response is spicy and defensive. I have seen all-out social media wars on topics like baby gender reveal parties (sure, why not?) and how toilet paper should be placed on the roll (over, of course). The wars involving light topics end up being entertaining and don't really hurt anyone, but when worldviews or issues involving social justice join the mix, things get truly heated.

That might be because your worldview is probably the most important thing about you, even if you don't think about it like that. You are defined by what you believe. So, when someone says something against your faith or beliefs, it cuts right to the gut. I'm not talking about debates about nonsalvific (secondary, gray) issues; rather, I'm talking about when someone mocks the very core of your belief—that God isn't real or that Jesus was never resurrected—the very foundations of your faith.

Speaking of Jesus, think about all He endured on His way to death, which, incidentally, was brought about at the hands of the very people who had claimed to worship Him just days before. He was mocked by Jewish people and Gentiles. People spit on Him. He was mocked by Roman soldiers who clothed Him in the color of royalty, placed a crown of thorns on His head, and had Him hold a staff (like a king would hold a scepter). He was beaten in the most tortuous way. Then, as He was dying on the cross, He was mocked by the crowd, which included priests, soldiers, and other people. And yet, Jesus asked His Father to forgive them. He didn't even try to defend Himself.

In light of what happened to Jesus, we shouldn't be surprised that people are mocking our faith, the one founded by Him. In fact, Peter warned the early Christians "that in the last days scoffers will come, scoffing and following their own evil desires" (2 Peter 3:3). He had experienced mockery at the hands of unbelievers shortly after Jesus' arrest, so he certainly understood what he was talking about. Jude echoed Peter's sentiment in his epistle, warning against the people who work to divide believers (verses 17-22). Knowing it will happen doesn't make it easier to take, but it should help us understand that we don't need to defend ourselves. Instead, we should be able to defend why we believe what we believe.

This is where apologetics can be helpful. Having evidence for our beliefs can help us take things less personally. Perhaps we'll determine that a response isn't necessary—I think that's true a lot, and we should be okay with staying silent. But perhaps engaging in a conversation with those who mock your faith can prove fruitful in the end. You'll need to ask the Holy Spirit which direction you should go in particular instances. He wants to be your helper—let Him.

BE QUICK TO FORGIVE

At the risk of sounding like a superfan of the show (I might be, at least of Season 1), I'm going to use another example from *Ted Lasso*. The show features a kitman (equipment manager) turned assistant coach named Nate (aka the Wonder Kid and Nate the Great). Nate lets his pride get the best of him, and he ends up destroying an important team symbol to make a point.

The final season shows Nate's redemption story—he receives grace and forgiveness from the coaching staff as well as the team itself. He didn't earn it, but they still gave it to him. Perhaps one of the reasons why scenes like this strike such a chord with viewers is because we yearn to see it happen in real life. Despite the example Christ gave us on the cross, dying for our sins even when we didn't deserve it, it seems that we mere mortals don't find forgiveness easy.

In a 2019 Barna survey, 76 percent of Christian respondents said they are quick to offer unconditional forgiveness, but only 55 percent said that they have been unconditionally forgiven by someone else. An astonishing 38 percent said they have never received unconditional forgiveness from another person.[8] The Barna report suggests the disparity exists because "the perceptions of giving versus receiving unconditional forgiveness may sometimes vary dramatically—meaning, while someone may feel they have extended unconditional forgiveness, the supposed recipient of that forgiveness may not feel the same way."[9] One more somewhat shocking result of the survey was that 60 percent of Christians said they can name a person they are having a tough time forgiving, and 23 percent said there is someone in their life that they cannot forgive.

However, Scripture makes it clear that we are called to forgive: "Bear with each other and forgive one another if any of you has a grievance against someone. Forgive as the Lord forgave you. And over all these virtues put on love, which binds them all together in perfect unity" (Colossians 3:13-14). Jesus called us to a higher standard than eye for an eye; we're supposed to turn the other cheek (see Matthew 5:38-39). Jesus also boldly proclaimed that we should love our enemies—"do good to them, and lend to them without expecting to get anything back" (Luke 6:35). There aren't any caveats that come with the mandate. No one gets a free pass here.

Someone says something cruel to you because of your beliefs? Offer forgiveness. Someone vandalizes your church? Offer forgiveness. Someone tries to kill you because you're a Christian? Offer forgiveness. To be clear, I am in no way implying that each of these scenarios is the same or that forgiveness should be offered with no consequences for the wrongful act. Indeed, our Father is a just God, but He also extends grace and mercy. There should be a balance of justice and forgiveness. When there are situations where justice is necessary, a willingness to forgive should also be present.

If you choose to engage with someone who has mocked you or attempted to harm you because of your faith, be willing to extend mercy, just as Jesus asked the Father to forgive those who mocked and killed Him. We're not at war with people; we are at war with false ideologies, and our desire should always be to show people hope. Remember Paul's words to the Ephesians: "Get rid of all bitterness, rage and anger, brawling and slander, along with every form of malice. Be kind and compassionate to one another, forgiving each other, just as in Christ God forgave you" (Ephesians 4:31-32).

When I was growing up, I learned that I shouldn't point at people because at least two fingers were pointing back at me. Silly, when you really think about it, but it does make sense when we're talking about judgment, mercy, and forgiveness. Although offering forgiveness can be tough, it can be even more difficult to admit when we're in the wrong. Jesus warned His disciples about this in Matthew 7 when He talked about judging others. He didn't mince words: "You hypocrite, first take the plank out of your own eye, and then you will see clearly to remove the speck from your brother's eye" (verse 5). As Christians, we need to take a long, hard look at the planks in our own eyes, including our inclinations to make fun of beliefs we find strange.

RELIGION AND HUMOR

"Where's your sense of humor? It was just a joke!" When someone gets offended by a joke that cuts to the core of who they are, it's not easy for them to let it go without comment. When religion gets involved, the situation often gets sticky. Yet comedians use religion as the butt of the joke because it makes people laugh, even if it's offensive. It's not only Christianity they are after, either. The South Park writers have gone after everyone from Latter-day Saints to Scientologists. Late-night comedians and stand-up comedians go after Muslims, Christians, Jewish people, and even atheists. Typically, the jokes are about stereotypes of religious/antireligious people, and typically, the audience is completely on board. To be fair, they probably knew what they were signing up for when they bought the ticket.

It seems comedians can get away with making fun of peoples' beliefs and worldviews—especially in America, where "free speech" is a right. In fact, that excuse is used to support this type of comedy pretty often, and the support isn't just from nonreligious people. One person defended religious comedy in this way:

> This is America, for crying out loud! I absolutely love it that comedians can joke about anything and everything. It's a matter of free speech. And if you can't laugh at stereotypes of your own faith, maybe you ought to do a little soul-searching.[10]

What about satire? Satire is when we use irony to ridicule ideas, people, or people groups. It's often funny because there is a hint of truth in the headline or the story. Perhaps the most popular satirical site online is *The Onion*, but there are also Christian-owned sites like *The Babylon Bee* and *Lutheran Satire*. It can be easy to forget the purpose behind satire and jump on the bandwagon of making fun of others and their beliefs. Is satire a Christian practice? It depends. What's the heart behind the headline, and what's the effect on the reader? If it's just to mock people, that's a no-go.[11] Is it twisting reality and convincing people of falsehood? We should probably avoid it. However, if satire is being used to call out falsehood in a funny way without causing the listener to stumble by mocking their neighbor for holding such false beliefs, then it's likely okay.

Lutheran Satire, for example, often creates YouTube videos featuring Donall and Conall, who discuss different worldviews through conversations with particular animated people, such as Latter-day Saint missionaries or Saint Patrick. The conversations typically begin with them asking questions and then poking holes in the falsehoods professed in the answers given. They are funny and well-executed. They get at the heart of what is wrong about specific worldviews, even poking fun at some of the silly ways we as Christians have messed things up (see their video about the Trinity).

Ultimately, humor can be used to lighten the mood or even to reveal the truth. It must be done with Christian character, though. We shouldn't use ad hominem (personal) attacks. Our hope should always be to reveal God's kingdom here on Earth, making disciples. If what we say, even if it's funny, leads people away, we simply shouldn't participate. I think this is a good time to remind everyone of the Golden Rule: "In everything, do to others what you would have them do to you, for this sums up the Law and the Prophets" (Matthew 7:12). If Christians don't want others to make fun of Christianity, Christians shouldn't make fun of other worldviews. It's really as simple as that.

Some awful things have been said by Christians against others. Even as individuals, we make mistakes—we treat people with unkindness, we expect forgiveness without offering it freely to others. A simple way to build bridges is to evaluate your life for anything that is inconsistent with the gospel and remove it. Then, extend forgiveness. Give it without reservation or expectation.

CHOOSE JOY

There's a caveat to all this, and it has to do with humor. Generally, I am not a funny person (I don't crack a lot of jokes), but I do appreciate humor in TV shows, films, and the occasional *Dry Bar Comedy* episode. It's okay to enjoy funny things. It's okay to laugh at ourselves, and it's okay, even, to find some jokes about religion funny. G.K. Chesterton once quipped that "it is the test of a good religion whether you can joke about it."[12] Indeed, it is not all that unusual for theologians and apologists to use humor to put their listeners' minds at ease or even to drive home a theological point.[13]

It appears God Himself has a sense of humor. God has used humor through His prophets to send a message to His people. For example, Elijah's interaction with the prophets of Baal in 1 Kings 18 is rife with satire—he challenges them to make their god appear, and when that doesn't happen, Elijah asks if their god is "deep in thought, or busy, or traveling. Maybe he is sleeping and must be awakened" (verse 27). Then he summons the Lord, who responds (verses 37-38). Our God wasn't too busy to show up when His people needed Him. He wasn't asleep or too absorbed with philosophizing about the world.

Just as Elijah showed the prophets of Baal, humor can be a great lesson builder. During the pandemic, I participated in a series of You-Tube videos called "Quality Quarantine," which featured Mama Bear Apologetics and Elizabeth Urbanowicz from Foundation Worldview. In one episode, we featured sock puppets to show that we could use something silly to talk about things like emotions with children.[14] Humor can break down barriers and build bridges, but it must be done well and without the goal of belittling and demeaning anyone. There's a fine line that shouldn't be crossed.

BUILDING THE BRIDGE

Getting made fun of for any reason isn't something any of us look forward to, and it isn't funny to be the reason behind a joke, especially if it's because of something as valuable to you as your faith. Sometimes, of course, you'll find jokes (even those about Christianity) funny. But if you are hurt by what is said, you have a few choices. In some instances, like when you don't really know the person, it might be best to simply move on without engaging. It may also be helpful to recognize that perhaps the other person has never met a Christian who has been kind to them. Or perhaps they had a bad experience with Christianity or the church and its people. The joke probably isn't about you personally, even though it feels that way.

In instances when you know the person, graciously let them know how you feel. Respond with gentleness, not in-kind (don't succumb to the ad hominem, or personal, attack). If a friend or coworker is mocking your beliefs, ask them why they think the joke is funny. You can also, in a polite way, ask them to stop. If they don't, the simplest thing to do is probably to walk away. It won't mean the friendship is over, of course, but doing this will allow you to catch your breath and think before you blurt out words of anger or hurt. Bridges are built with a wide variety of experiences, including ones that aren't fun in the moment. The bridge isn't broken; it has a crack, and cracks can be repaired. To repair it, you can plan a time to discuss your thoughts about humor and religion with your friends and let them know that you don't want to participate in that kind of behavior.

Bridge builders can set up boundaries (see chapter 13). Ultimately, we want to show people Jesus, and remaining calm in spite of our hurt will set us up for a successful bridge repair.

QUESTIONS FOR REFLECTION AND DISCUSSION

1. Have you ever been made fun of for your beliefs? If so, how did you respond?

2. What's the best way we can defend Jesus when someone mocks Christianity?

3. Is there someone you need to forgive who has offended you because of your worldview?

4. Do you need to ask anyone for forgiveness for mocking their worldview?

5. Think about how you've seen Christians portrayed by Hollywood. Is their portrayal consistent with what you know about how Christians (should) behave?

RECOMMENDED RESOURCES

Steve Wilkens, *What's So Funny About God?: A Theological Look at Humor* (Westmont, IL: IVP Academic, 2019)

Peter Kreeft, *Ha!: A Christian Philosophy of Humor* (South Bend, IN: St. Augustine's Press, 2022)

13

WHEN BARRIERS ARE NECESSARY—GUARDRAILS AND BUMPERS

The way to love anything is to realize that it may be lost.

G.K. CHESTERTON

We used to live in Colorado, and we've ascended Pikes Peak in Colorado Springs a few times. By ascend, I mean by car, not by hiking, though many people do hike the 14,000-foot mountain, for fun, by the way. Once you're at the top, it is amazing to get out, take in the incredible view (you can see five states from the summit!), and have one of the mountaintop café's world-famous high-altitude donuts (which deflate when you return to the bottom of the peak).

Getting to the top of Pikes Peak used to be a bit more dangerous than it is today because until recently, much of the narrow roadway was unpaved. That's not the scariest part, though. Even today, there are quite a few spots with no guardrails. The idea is that you will take your time, and eventually, you'll make it to the top. In fact, it will take you about two to three hours to complete the 38-mile round trip. You'll also go through about half a tank of gas. Slow and steady wins the race.

Well, not exactly on Pikes Peak, where astonishingly, there is an annual race to the top that has been taking place since 1916—cars racing along narrow roads, up to a 14,000-foot summit, with very few guardrails. The record for speed is held by Frenchman Romain Dumas, who ascended the mountain in less than eight minutes in his electric Volkswagen in 2018. Talk about thrilling! There is a definite risk involved—seven people have died attempting the harrowing race to the top, but that doesn't stop the adventurers from continuing the tradition year in and year out. It's exciting. It's dangerous. And to me, it's just plain crazy, but to each their own.

Most dangerous roadways and bridges have guardrails. Guardrails help keep us from falling off the ledge to certain death. People bridges need guardrails too. Sometimes we need to let relationships go so we can protect ourselves and our well-being. I don't think this should be a regular habit, but when necessary, you should put up guardrails.

There are other times when we don't need full-blown guardrails but bumpers, like the ones kids (and some adults!) use while bowling. Bumpers provide some brief respite when things start to go off the rail. Bumpers keep you safe and on track. This chapter will give you some help for the times when you find yourself in a place where you need to put up some guardrails or bumpers. It will also help you understand when you can let the bumpers down and navigate without them.

WHEN TO PUT UP A GUARDRAIL

Sometimes we need boundaries. Scripture tells us, "Above all else, guard your heart, for everything you do flows from it" (Proverbs 4:23). Guess what? Even Jesus exercised His right to boundaries. Luke 5:16 says, "Jesus often withdrew to lonely places and prayed." He did this at a time when His ministry was at its peak, when throngs of people were visiting Him from near and far. He needed to get away at times, and that was okay.

Boundaries are not walls; they're more like fences. Sometimes they'll need to be elevated from a white picket fence with a gate to a chain link fence with a lock, but boundaries are still navigable. We may need to set boundaries in place if we feel unsafe in a friendship or if we are being harmed in some way. Boundaries can also be helpful when we need a breather, a moment to consider a relationship and take care of our own emotions and attitudes, whatever they may be.

Keep in mind that friends will inevitably disagree about things—that's often one of the more challenging *and* rewarding aspects of having close friends. But in the times when the interaction gets to be too much, you may need to take a break. We see this in Scripture with Paul and Barnabas in Acts. They had both been traveling and spreading the gospel together, but then they reached an impasse over John Mark. This led to their decision to part ways, Barnabas leaving with John Mark, and Paul leaving with Silas (see Acts 15:36-41).

Despite the tension, it seems like there was reconciliation at some point because Paul mentions Barnabas and John Mark in his various letters. In his commentary on Acts, Ajith Fernando notes that Paul and Barnabas serve as a reminder that "because God is greater than the problem, we can always live with hope of resolution. That hope will enable us to look beyond the hurt to the day when we will rejoice in a relationship restored."[1] Indeed, when we are kingdom minded and willing to step away from earthly commitments to serve in the way God has commanded us to serve, we leave the door open for hope in all things. We may not see such reconciliation happen here on earth, but eternity is but a breath away.

When enforcing boundaries with friends, it may be helpful to set a limit on such breaks, if necessary, establishing a time when you'll come back together for a chat over coffee (or tea). Even if things get truly bad, try to leave open the opportunity for reconciliation, as it seems happened with Paul and Barnabas. If that is not possible due to specific circumstances, allow yourself time to reflect and forgive. You may also need to come to terms with the fact that your boundary in those types of situations means that your friendship may never recover. Grieve as much as you need to about the loss and give your worry to the Lord, who cares for you deeply (Psalm 55:22).

I'd like to give a gentle reminder that boundaries shouldn't be used just to avoid hard things in a friendship. In a podcast, Jackie Hill Perry said she checks herself when she feels like she needs to put a boundary in place. "I need to interrogate if I'm setting up a boundary because it's the wise thing to do," she said, "or if I'm using it as an excuse to preserve my own comforts."[2]

It might seem as though that's what happened with Paul and Barnabas—that things got difficult, so they abandoned one another. But try looking at it another way. Paul had mentored Barnabas for as long as he could, and Barnabas had started to lead rather than follow. This was a natural progression of their friendship. Yes, their fight resulted in a physical boundary of distance, but they both continued to heed the calling God had placed on their lives. They may have disagreed, but it's possible the separation would have occurred soon anyway. And they probably came back together at some point. They didn't speak poorly about one another, nor did they try to destroy one another's ministries.

Which brings me back to love. In their best-selling book *Boundaries*, Henry Cloud and John Townsend write that "at any moment, any person can walk away from a friendship. However, as we enter more and more into an attachment-based life, we learn to trust love."[3] Mutual love between friends means that you'll respect one another's feelings. You'll also extend each other grace and mercy. You'll desire reconciliation and avoid gossip and ill will toward one another. Boundaries don't have to be forever, especially when love is a part of the equation.

BUMPERS ARE ENCOURAGED (EVEN FOR ADULTS!)

When I turned eight, some friends came over to my house, and then we went bowling. During that experience, I got to see what happens to the pins and balls behind the scenes, and I learned the value of bumpers. Bumpers help keep the bowling ball on course so that it doesn't fall into the gutter. They are usually used by young children, but I know an adult (or two or three) who still use them when they bowl—I promise you're getting absolutely no judgment from me!

Did you know that bridges have bumpers too? Bridge bumpers are more like the bumpers you find on cars and trucks—that is, they help absorb the impact during collisions. Sometimes people bridges need bumpers too. In this context, bumpers can look like prayer warriors, mentors, and other Christians in your everyday life. They provide encouragement, they help you develop skills and gifts used in bridge building, and they pray for you often. When a people-bridge-building bumper (say that three times fast!) supports you, you are lifted up and inspired to stick with God's truth in all interactions. Such bumpers also help to absorb the impact when we traverse difficult paths, whether the impact is self-inflicted or brought about by outside forces.

The first bumper you can put in your life is a Bible-teaching church. A church that takes the Word of God seriously and believes in the transforming power of prayer. A church that motivates its attendees to love others the way Jesus does. A church that shows compassion to the "least of these" (a la Matthew 25:40-45). The Bible encourages us to meet with other Christians for these very reasons:

> Let us hold unswervingly to the hope we profess, for he who promised is faithful. And let us consider how we may spur one another on toward love and good deeds, not giving up meeting together, as some are in the habit of doing, but encouraging one another—and all the more as you see the Day approaching (Hebrews 10:23-25).

As I touched on in chapter 8, going to church is good for you. Not only are you speaking with other believers and experiencing spiritual growth through worship and Bible teaching, you often also tend to have life experiences with friends from church, like serving in the community together or spending time in small groups with each other.[4] It gets even better, though.

In a 2020 study of 100,000 health-care professionals, men who attended religious services at least once per week were 33 percent less likely to die of despair (involving drugs, alcohol, or suicide), while women were 68 percent less likely than those who did not attend regular religious services.[5] Although the study was limited to health-care professionals and there was no specification as to type of religion practiced, the numbers still illustrate that meeting together with other believers is beneficial.

Another great bumper is a Christian mentor—someone with more experience and wisdom than you. In the situation involving Paul and Barnabas, there was both a boundary and a bumper.[6] Mentoring is when a person with specific skills shares their knowledge and experience with another to help them grow in those areas. Typically this is an older person with a younger person, but that doesn't have to be the case, especially in instances where spiritual maturity matters.

In seminary, I was required to have a mentor who helped me with certain areas of my life, whether it was spiritual, emotional, or practical. The first year, my mentor was someone who had experienced adoption and could speak into my life in that area, mentoring me as an adoptive mom and helping me navigate the world of adoption. The next year, I asked my philosophy professor, Sarah Geis, to mentor me in all things writing. I needed someone to help me navigate the different types of writing styles and assist me in research methods as well as audience-specific approaches. That year was transformative for me. Sarah was (and continues to be) a bumper for me as I work to build bridges with other people, always ready with an encouraging word. She also holds me accountable when it seems like I'm off track, just like a bumper does to a bowling ball.

A mentor can provide the accountability you need to ensure that your bridge-building efforts are not done with wrong motives. A good mentor can also help you navigate the waters of boundaries and reconciliation should the need arise. If you don't have a mentor, I highly recommend you find someone who is willing to commit to your continued transformation through Christ. Finding a mentor who can help you with issues of truth and friendship can be especially helpful as you do your bridge building.

The final bumper in bridge building is prayer. Now, I realize that we already covered prayer in chapter 1, but we don't want to forget its place in building bridges with others. You'll need guidance as far as when to put boundaries in place and who to approach for mentoring. You'll also need to ask the Holy Spirit for direction as you choose a church or small group (see chapter 15).

BUILDING THE BRIDGE

As we wrap up this section, I thought it would be good to close with prayer because boundaries and guardrails are no small things. They are important to the sound structure of the bridges we build with people. Pastor and blogger Peter Englert wrote a prayer specifically for bridge builders that touches on boundaries and guardrails, and I thought it would be good to share it with you as you continue your journey.

> Lord, help us build bridges.
> We seem so polarized in the world today.
> Finding common ground seems impossible.
> Grace and truth seem so far apart.
> The distance from others grows and grows.

Through the cross, You tore down the wall that divided us.
You reconciled us to yourself and each other.
Let us start by first seeing Your image in each other.
May the Church become an agent of peace and healing.
We realize that only You can bring people near
    who live far apart.

Give us the courage to become bridgebuilders.
Let us be those who stand in the gap.
May we minister to the hurting and grieving.
Walk with us in the spaces of those who don't see
    eye to eye.
Guide in conversation to listen well.
We pray to bless our enemies.

You have brought people together who only had the
    gospel in common.
So today, we walk in Your grace and mercy.
Transform our hearts and minds.
We lean on You to build the bridges that we never
    thought would be built.
Our hope and trust is in You alone. Amen[7]

QUESTIONS FOR REFLECTION AND DISCUSSION

1. Have you ever avoided a collision or life-altering accident because of guardrails?

2. What boundaries do you currently have in place that can help you with bridge building?

3. What boundaries do you need to put in place to guard your heart?

4. Do you have a mentor? If so, how does having one help you? If not, consider someone in your life whom you could ask to mentor you with regard to spiritual, emotional, or practical matters.

5. Is there a younger person in your church you could mentor? What could you offer as a mentor?

RECOMMENDED RESOURCES

Henry Cloud and John Townsend, *Boundaries* (Grand Rapids, MI: Zondervan, 2017)

Timothy Keller and John Inazu, *Uncommon Ground: Living Faithfully in a World of Difference* (Nashville, TN: Thomas Nelson, 2020)

Barnabas Piper, *Belong: Loving Your Church by Reflecting Christ to One Another* (Charlotte, NC: The Good Book Company, 2023)

Mark Mittelberg, *Contagious Faith* (Grand Rapids, MI: Zondervan, 2021)

CONFIDENTLY SHARING YOUR FAITH

Our faith becomes stronger as we express
it; a growing faith is a sharing faith.

BILLY GRAHAM

When was the last time you shared your faith with someone? First Peter 3:15 states that you should expect opportunities to give a defense for the hope within you. Does the mere thought of doing that make you weak in the knees? Can you feel your pulse increasing and your heart pounding? You're not alone.

This is a book about building bridges, which implies that we are going to take those bridges somewhere. We're connecting to people. Otherwise, why would we build anything? I said in the introduction of this book that we are not entering into missional relationships solely with the intention of sharing the gospel, but what happens when the opportunity presents itself, or a friend, family member, coworker, or neighbor asks you about your faith? This chapter will help you put together everything you've learned thus far in this book and hope-fully give you some courage to openly and confidently share your beliefs with others.

KNOW THE HOPE WITHIN YOU

I'd be remiss if I didn't bring up our hope once more. The fifth lesson from Jesus (see chapter 5) was to offer hope. It's what He did. It's what His disciples did. And it's what we're called to do. He is the hope of the world, and we can't forget that. Bridge building can seem daunting at times, I'm sure, but with the hope of Jesus (the gospel) at front and center of our relationships with others, laying bricks becomes a little easier. We mustn't forget the mission to love God and love others.

Loving God includes remembering all that He's done for us—especially sending Jesus to live among us, teach us His ways, die a terrible death, be resurrected on the third day, and ascend to heaven to await our reunion when the Father says it's time. If it helps, remind yourself of the gospel message every day. Thank God for His Son, and when you say it, mean it. Consider all that Jesus did and why. For you. For your salvation. For your reconciliation with God. I believe that if we fully digest the gospel message, we won't struggle to talk about our hope with others. We'll be too excited to stay silent, sort of like that kid in the Disney commercial who is too excited to sleep because he's going to Disney the next day.

Friend, we have but a few tomorrows left before we are joined with the community of saints from all generations in eternity. It's okay to be excited about that. But…we're not there yet. As Craig Blomberg constantly reminded my New Testament class, we're living in the already and not yet. We can be excited about it, but we can't forget our mission, our goal—to be kingdom minded with a priority of instilling hope (Jesus) in a fallen world that is in desperate need of a Savior.

To know the hope within you and to really value what it means to be kingdom minded, you need to be in Scripture, prayer, and fellowship with other believers. Study the Word so that you understand the Word. I'm not saying you need to go to seminary. There are books and podcasts and devotionals that can help, many of which I recommended in this book. There are seminaries that offer certificates in different areas of study like the New Testament or apologetics. There are also studies available through RightNow Media. And don't underestimate the value of a good study Bible with substantial footnotes and commentary. Finally, your church might offer special classes about the Bible or prayer. Join one and learn with and from other Christians. Encourage one another and persist in the faith together. Then do as Jesus said: "Go and make disciples of all nations, baptizing them in the name of the Father and of the Son and of the Holy Spirit, and teaching them to obey everything I have commanded you. And surely I am with you always, to the very end of the age" (Matthew 28:19-20).

AN ETHIC OF LOVE

Throughout this book, I've noted some difficulties for Christians when it comes to evangelism, including our ability to be in relationship with people who think and behave differently than we do. The foundation of these friendships is truth, and the foundation for Christian living is becoming like Christ. We are no longer bound under the law of the Old Testament; instead, we are united under Christ. Indeed, as Scott Rae describes in his book *Moral Choices*, Jesus and His disciples "take the central command of the Law, 'Love the Lord your God with all your heart and with all your soul and with all your strength' (Deut. 6:5), and develop an ethic of love for God and one's neighbor."[1] Rae goes so far as to say that "love is considered the ultimate expression of the virtues involved in following Jesus and the indicator of how substantial the commitment to one's faith is."[2]

Recall that Paul said in 1 Corinthians 13:1 that without love we are "a resounding gong or a clanging cymbal" (see chapter 6). The type of love described in 1 Corinthians 13 is *agape*—that is, the highest form of love mentioned in all of Scripture. The English word *love* doesn't do it justice. Craig Blomberg explains that "love is first of all an action, an unconditional commitment, a promise that is never broken."[3] Love, then, is an outward expression of our faith. Without a living and breathing faith in the promise of Christ as our Savior, we cannot show genuine love. But we must not overthink it—instead, the more we live it, the more natural it becomes.

JUST BREATHE

When you've entered a conversation and the subject of faith comes up, take a deep breath and settle in for the ride. It's amazing what a good cleansing breath or two can do for our systems.[4] Plus, taking a deep breath buys you some time to think through some things and pray. Interestingly, your manner of breathing can also help the person you're speaking with have confidence in the words you're saying. In fact, former opera singer and diplomatic speechwriter Allison Shapira says that "the ability to harness your breath is one of the most important and least taught areas within public speaking."[5] Breathing, she notes, is "one of the key elements of executive presence."[6] So breathing isn't just a tool you can use to calm yourself down and gather your thoughts; it can actually change the way people perceive your words. The right kind of breathing is powerful.

BEING HOSPITABLE CAN CHANGE LIVES

One simple way to confidently share your faith through love is to show hospitality toward your neighbors. You might be thinking to yourself, especially if you're female, that this is about to become a lecture about how to welcome people into your home. No, there are already excellent books on the topic. You might also be quietly panicking on the inside (please don't toss this book across the room) because you can't imagine inviting people over. Relax, and don't throw hospitality out the window because you think it's old fashioned or only for women. Hospitality is a wonderful way to open your arms and serve others well.

While we were in seminary, Jay and I had the great privilege of getting to know Gordon and Gail MacDonald. Their apartment was right across from ours, and when they were in town, they always selected one evening during their visit to invite us over for dessert and coffee. I will treasure those moments forever because the MacDonalds took the time to get to know us and encourage us. They often shared with us how they interacted with, prayed for, and cared for others. Their apartment was always stocked with coffee *and* tea because sometimes their visitors didn't like coffee. And over pie and warm drinks, Jay and I learned about hospitality. During one such visit, Gail gave me a copy of her book *High Call, High Privilege*. In it, she writes about the importance of hospitality versus merely entertaining:

> Hospitality is a safe place, entertainment is a show place. Hospitality focuses on people, entertainment focuses on things. Hospitality creates an open atmosphere, entertainment can be neat and closed. Hospitality exudes a warm attitude, entertainment can degenerate to being cool and calculating. Hospitality puts one at ease, entertainment implies competition.[7]

Each time we visited, the MacDonalds asked about things we had talked about during prior visits. After we left, they took notes in their journals so that they could continue to pray for us while they were away. And their hospitality extended beyond the walls of their apartment—we received many handwritten notes from them, and we continue to receive emails to check in on us. Hospitality can enrich the lives of the people around us, and it helps create a place where conversation and genuine relationship are not only imagined but experienced.

Rosaria Butterfield recently wrote a book titled *The Gospel Comes with a House Key*, in which she chronicles how hospitality shifted her worldview. She was an outspoken lesbian when Ken and Floy Smith, a pastor and his wife, invited her over for dinner. She had plans to learn from them, but not in a Christian sense. Rosaria initially thought of her visits to their home as an opportunity to gain inside information about Christians—she called it "the cult house" to her friends.[8] She was going to use what she learned from them against them and other Christians.

Eventually, however, Ken and Floy's sincere kindness chipped away at the barriers Rosaria had set up against them. She was fed both spiritually and physically in their home. She felt safe enough to share honestly and openly with them. And she did this despite the fact that Ken told her they accepted her but did not approve of her actions in life. There's a distinction, in other words, between love and affirmation of sin. Ken and Floy persisted in their love toward Rosaria but never wavered on the truth. This is what Francis Schaeffer referred to as part of the evidence of Christianity in one's life in *The Mark of the Christian*: "So often people think that Christianity is only something soft, only a kind of gooey love that loves evil equally with good," he wrote. "This is not the biblical position. The holiness of God is to be exhibited simultaneously with love."[9] Ultimately, Butterfield's life was radically transformed due to, at least in part, the Smiths's faithfulness to hospitality, love, and truth.[10]

What's important to remember about inviting people to dinner is that you're not offering them entertainment. Instead, you're welcoming them into your home with warmth and openness. Kind of like State Farm's catchphrase, "Like a good neighbor, State Farm is there." You're being there for your neighbors. This does not mean that you need to present the perfect home and the perfect meal. Remember, you are not entertaining. Think of the occasion as an opportunity to welcome people into your life. Your life probably doesn't always look like mopped floors, dusted bookshelves, or even an empty kitchen sink. I'm not saying you shouldn't pick up a little (Legos hurt, so clean them up!), but don't present a false version of yourself when you're trying to build bridges and genuine friendships. Eventually, others are going to find out that you occasionally leave dishes in the sink or that you simply don't give a second thought to that dust on your bookshelves. And that's okay.

My husband and I hosted a small group in our home a couple of years ago. I was convinced, at least at the beginning, that our home had to be perfect when people came over. Of course, perfect means that the piles of mail and other papers move from the kitchen table to a forbidden closet of doom, where all the unsightly things go, never to be seen again. But eventually, as our friendships deepened with the members of our small group, the messiness wasn't as big a concern. We'd move the dirty dishes into the dishwasher, but the counters were rarely wiped down and the piles of paper were simply shuffled to a portion of the counter we didn't need. And guess what? People stopped coming. No, no, I'm kidding. People kept coming, and no one ever said anything. We enjoyed our conversations and our friendships, despite the dust and paperwork.

So, too, will it likely be for you. Don't be afraid to invite a friend over simply because you don't have time or the willpower to do a deep clean of your home first. Make your home presentable (so that you at least have space at the table to eat and drink), but a welcoming home is more important than a perfect home. Trust me, the façade will fade eventually, your guests will see the real thing, and they'll still want to be around you, so long as you love well, care deeply, and have a real desire to know them. Building bridges doesn't require perfection; it requires a willingness to open your doors and hearts to your neighbors.

QUICK TO LISTEN, SLOW TO SPEAK

One of the links I've noticed between my experiences with the Mac-Donalds and Butterfield's experiences with the Smiths is that the ones offering hospitality were good listeners who patiently worked to understand the perspectives of their guests. They asked insightful (albeit sometimes challenging) questions that yielded trust and openness. They were safe. Often, we get so caught up in thinking about what we're going to say next that we forget to really listen to the words spoken by our visitors.

Recently I was speaking with a friend of mine who used to teach communication in college. She required her speech students to keep a listening journal[11] so that they would practice active listening. I think that is a great idea, and it is one many of us should adopt in our own lives. A listening journal can help us improve our conversation skills by giving us an opportunity to reflect on discussions we have had with others. Here are some questions you can consider as you endeavor to keep your own listening journal:

1. Who were you talking with?

2. What was the main topic?

3. How did you show the other person that you were actively listening (nodding, affirmative words, leaning in, etc.)?

4. How did you feel before, during, and after the conversation?

5. What questions did you ask?

By listening well, we can keep the conversation moving forward each time we meet. Active listening means we seek to understand and learn.

ASK GOOD QUESTIONS

Andy Bannister's book *How to Talk About Jesus Without Looking Like an Idiot* cuts to the heart of a lot of our worries—we don't talk about our faith because we don't want to look dumb to our friends. Bannister outlines the power of good questions, using the basics you probably learned in grade school: *what*, *why*, *whether*, and other *wondering* questions.[12] The good news is that questions can help with that by taking the load off our shoulders and putting the ball in the other person's court. You may be thinking that it's not that simple, but truly, it is. Remember, people enjoy talking about themselves.

A few years ago, I was traveling to Los Angeles for a conference. Armed with a Coke and a book, I settled in for the flight. Then the lady next to me asked me if I was a Scientologist. Perhaps she was prompted by the book I was reading (a book clearly about Scientology based on its title), and she was probably unimpeded to ask the question because I didn't have any headphones on. Of course, I told her no and let her know I was a Christian, and almost immediately after she asked if I was a Scientologist, I turned the tables and asked her about her own faith.

For the next two hours, she and I talked about religion, philosophy, cults, California weather, and more. It was a give-and-take situation. Her boldness led to a lovely conversation that sparked my interest and hers. We were connected that day, even though we'll probably never see each other again. And yet, seeds were planted, in my life and probably in hers. I often think about her willingness to enter the potential fray by asking a question about my faith. Sometimes we're held back because we're afraid we'll offend someone with a question. But rarely are people upset when we ask them questions about themselves, and then often, they want to learn more about us in return.

So what kinds of questions can we ask? Here are a few suggestions:

- What do you believe about faith and spirituality?

- Do you believe there is a God? If so, what's His role?

- What do you think happens when we die?

- What is sin, and how does it affect humanity?

- How do you find joy?

- Where does your hope come from?

Now, these questions are philosophical and in some ways quite heady. It is probably best to let the conversation guide you as far as specific questions to ask. For example, if you're on a plane going through turbulence, that's probably not the time to ask about death and eternity, but it could be a good opportunity to ask what brings that person joy or hope.

If you ask questions, you can almost guarantee that you will also be asked questions. Here are some that could arise about your faith while you're bridge building:

- How do you know the Bible is true?

- Should we take the Bible seriously?

- Why did you become a Christian?

- Where does your hope come from?

- Why does it matter whether we go to church?

- If God is all good, why is there evil in the world?

You'll notice some overlap between the first set of questions and the next, and of course, there could be even more similarities in the conversations you have with others. It depends on the context of your discussions. You should at least be familiar with the questions you could get asked about your beliefs, and if you can't answer the questions, go to some recommended resources that can help you. It is extremely likely that no one will expect you to have all the answers, especially if you approach the talk with humility and kindness. Unless you're participating in a debate, you probably won't need to worry too much about hostility.

Speaking of kindness, I think it is a brick in and of itself. Be known for your kindness and generosity. Don't seek recognition for it, but instead, give the glory to Christ for instilling His character within you and for being the model you follow. Kindness will break through barriers when nothing else will. Don't underestimate its usefulness in bridge building.

Courage also plays a role in bridge building. It takes courage to put yourself out there. That is probably a key factor as to why evangelistic activity is at such a low in the US. A 2016 Lifeway Research poll found that although 47 percent of unchurched Americans said they would be willing to speak openly about their beliefs with others, only 29 percent said that a Christian had ever shared the gospel with them.[13] A survey from Jesus Film Project found that 22 percent of respondents didn't share their faith because they were afraid to, and 10 percent didn't feel equipped.[14] Be encouraged by the fact most people will not be offended if you share your faith with them, especially if there is a preexisting relationship. Be bold, brave, sincere, and kind.

BUILDING THE BRIDGE

One last warning: God's Word isn't your weapon against people. It's a weapon against falsehood, and it's powerful. Hebrews 4:12 says, "The word of God is alive and active. Sharper than any double-edged sword, it penetrates even to dividing soul and spirit, joints and marrow; it judges the thoughts and attitudes of the heart." We'll talk more about the sword of truth in chapter 15, but for now, recognize that you are called to be a witness for Christ, and His top two commandments for us are to love God and love people. He didn't tell us to destroy people. That's what Satan tries to do. As Christians, our strongest desire as bridge builders should be to lead others into Christ's open arms.

QUESTIONS FOR REFLECTION AND DISCUSSION

1. State the gospel in 30 seconds. We practiced doing this in an earlier challenge, so now you can figure out much you've grown and improved since you started reading this book.

2. What is the hope within you?

3. What's your favorite book of the Bible, and why?

4. If you could meet any person from the Bible, who would it be, and why?

5. In what ways do you get excited about bridge building? What makes you nervous? How can you overcome that nervousness?

RECOMMENDED RESOURCES

Rosaria Butterfield, *The Gospel Comes with a House Key* (Wheaton, IL: Crossway, 2018)

Os Guinness, *Fool's Talk: Recovering the Art of Christian Persuasion* (Westmont, IL: InterVarsity, 2015)

Amy Orr-Ewing, *Why Trust the Bible?: Answers to Ten Tough Questions*, rev. ed. (Westmont, IL: InterVarsity, 2020)

LEAVE ROOM FOR THE HOLY SPIRIT

If we rely on the Holy Spirit, we shall find that our prayers become more and more inarticulate; and when they are inarticulate, reverence grows deeper and deeper.

OSWALD CHAMBERS

magine a dance hosted by a Christian school in the late 1990s. Boys and girls gather along the walls, and then one or two brave couples step onto the dance floor while Boyz II Men croon about love. Then, just when the girl nestles in close, a teacher pulls the couple apart and reminds them to leave room for the Holy Spirit. I won't say this was my experience because I typically stuck to the walls at school dances (I'm an introvert through and through), but I know this happened to friends. Saving room for the Holy Spirit was a way of exhorting kids to not succumb to urges meant only for married couples. Yet the Holy Spirit is so much more than a guardian against our sexual impulses. He's God, and He is holy and powerful and our mediator. He's also a bit tough to understand for some (most) Christians. We know He's there, but we're not quite sure what to say about who He is or what He does for us.

Part of the reason is that we don't talk about Him much unless we "feel" something during a worship service—then we acknowledge

His presence. Yet He's already there. He's been there all along. He's neglected. Theologian Michael Bird explains that "too many churches are passionate for the glory of the Father, are resolute in their Christ-centered faith, but languish in a spiritual impoverishment by neglecting the Holy Spirit."[1] It's an atrocity, and it's leading believers to question whether the Holy Spirit is really part of the Christian Godhead. If He can't be explained, maybe He's not real.

Yes, in some ways, the Holy Spirit is difficult to comprehend, but that doesn't mean that He isn't real. Unfortunately, a recent survey from the Cultural Research Center at Arizona Christian University shows that a majority of American respondents believe "the Holy Spirit is not a living entity, but merely a symbol of God's power, presence or purity."[2] But Scripture says otherwise. The Bible tells us that the Holy Spirit is more than a force or a symbol; instead, the Holy Spirit is our *paraclete*, a Greek New Testament word that means He is our advocate. The Nicene Creed, one of Christianity's oldest and most widely accepted creeds, describes the Holy Spirit as "the Lord, the giver of life, who proceeds from the Father and the Son, who with the Father and the Son is adored and glorified, who has spoken through the prophets." These words are proclaimed weekly at church services by Christians all over the world.

But what does the Holy Spirit have to do with bridge building? *Everything*. He's our helper, our comforter, our peace. He's our wisdom, our understanding, our guide. He never leaves us. And it is important that He is the one who should guide every relationship we enter, every conversation we have, and every thought we possess. Bridge building, at its core, is engaging when the Holy Spirit prompts us to and trusting that He will guide the conversation. He's essential to evangelism. "The Holy Spirit acts in gospel preaching to evangelize, to execute God's purposes in our lives, and to impart to us an effervescent spiritual life,"[3] writes Bird.

Theologian Ajith Fernando shares Bird's sentiment: "The fullness of the Spirit is essential for Christian life and ministry."[4] Just as you wouldn't leave for a fishing trip without a fishing pole, you shouldn't leave without the Holy Spirit when doing kingdom work—that is, don't ever leave home without the Holy Spirit because your life is kingdom work. This chapter will remind you of the Holy Spirit's presence as well as help you keep Him at the center of all that you do for the kingdom of God.

PARACLETE—YOUR PERSONAL PARACHUTE

Would you jump out of a plane without a parachute? Probably not if you wanted to live longer than another minute. That same urgency should exist when you think about not equipping yourself with the Holy Spirit before you leave your home. Jesus knew His followers were going to need help when He departed, so He left us a life-giving *paraclete*. When Jesus first appeared to His disciples after His resurrection and before His ascension into heaven, "he breathed on them and said, 'Receive the Holy Spirit'" (John 20:22). Then He told His apostles that they would be baptized with the Holy Spirit and have power from the Spirit (Acts 1:5, 8).

THE EARLY CHURCH'S HOLY SPIRIT EXPERIENCE

Imagine you're one of the disciples, and you've just witnessed your friend, mentor, and Savior fly up into the sky and disappear (Acts 1:9). This, after He was clearly dead and came back to life a few days later. The disciples were probably on edge, wondering what could possibly happen next, and then whoosh! The Holy Spirit makes Himself known (Acts 2). He didn't do it subtly, either. Acts 2:2-3 says, "Suddenly a sound like the blowing of a violent wind came from heaven and filled the whole house where they were sitting. They saw what seemed to be tongues of fire that separated and came to rest on each of them." Not only that, they all started speaking a different language (verse 4).

Jesus had told the disciples they would be baptized with the Holy Spirit, but they probably imagined something like the dove that appeared when Jesus was baptized (Matthew 3:16). Jesus had also said that they would have power, but they probably thought this meant they would continue to heal people and see people transformed in Jesus' name. Remember, this is the group that still had questions after they witnessed Jesus' many miracles. I'm sure they had questions when the Holy Spirit showed up!

The Holy Spirit is necessary and a wonderful help for us as believers and bridge builders. It's simply impossible for us to build bridges without Him. And not only are we gifted with His power, but He also brought us some presents.

GIFTS AND FRUITS OF THE HOLY SPIRIT

In his first letter to the Corinthians, Paul described the various gifts that come from the Holy Spirit: wisdom, teaching, faith, healing, power, speaking God's Word, discernment, and speaking in and interpreting tongues (1 Corinthians 12:4-11). These gifts all work for the Lord. They are intended to equip us as His saints so that we can do what He has called us to do in the best way possible.

Paul also wrote to the Galatians about the Holy Spirit. He said that Christians are identified by the characteristics of the Holy Spirit:

> The fruit of the Spirit is love, joy, peace, forbearance, kindness, goodness, faithfulness, gentleness, and self-control. Against such things there is no law. Those who belong to Christ Jesus have crucified the flesh with its passions and desires. Since we live by the Spirit, let us keep in step with the Spirit. Let us not become conceited, provoking and envying each other (5:22-26).

In other words, we are marked by the Spirit, and we are enabled to bear fruit for the kingdom of God. The Spirit doesn't leave us to build bridges on our own.

LET THE HOLY SPIRIT LEAD YOU

When I was with our friends Heather and Troy last year, we started talking about evangelism and the Holy Spirit. Troy and I were both missionary kids, and Heather, Troy, my husband, and I all met at seminary, so it is not that unusual for us to talk theology when we get together. Troy's parents (rightly) taught him and other missionaries that they should ask the Holy Spirit for guidance each time they thought they might have the opportunity to share their faith with someone. A simple prayer like, "Holy Spirit, is now the right time to share my faith?" would do. We should never assume that the answer will be the same each time. Only the Holy Spirit knows a person's heart. If we think the Holy Spirit is prompting us to speak about our beliefs, we should ask Him for guidance.

One of the beautiful aspects of being part of a body of believers is that we all receive different gifts from the Holy Spirit—gifts that work together to build each other up and to give glory to God. When Paul explained the working of the Holy Spirit to the church in Corinth, he said, "Now to each one the manifestation of the Spirit is given for the common good. To one there is given through the Spirit a *message of wisdom*, to another a *message of knowledge* by means of the same Spirit" (1 Corinthians 12:7-8, emphasis added).

In other words, the Spirit might tell you to speak, or He might not. And if He does, He will give you the wisdom you need to know what to share and when. If you sense the Holy Spirit is telling you to do something, you should listen. There might be a time when you absolutely do not want to share your faith, yet you feel like you can't walk away from the opportunity. I recommend that you step into that space, even if you're reluctant. Do so humbly. Do so cautiously. But be bold, knowing that you are not alone. You have a helper, a *paraclete*. Let Him lead you.

LET THE HOLY SPIRIT EMPOWER YOU

The Holy Spirit didn't stop equipping people after the early church era. He continues to offer His gifts to us. We may not spend a lot of time talking about the Holy Spirit in church, but keep in mind that He has gifted you in some way or other, as promised in 1 Corinthians 12:7. We're not all going to have the same gifts, so don't start comparing yourself with other believers. Paul warns the Christians in Corinth about this:

> There is one body, but it has many parts. But all its many parts make up one body. It is the same with Christ. We were all baptized by one Holy Spirit. And so we are formed into one body. It didn't matter whether we were Jews or Gentiles, slaves or free people. We were all given the same Spirit to drink. So the body is not made up of just one part. It has many parts (1 Corinthians 12:12-14).

We are all various parts who are being used in different ways by the Lord. Though we are all engaged in bridge building, the way we go about it will look different for each of us. Also, we can use our gifts to help other believers, and we shouldn't become jealous about how others have been gifted. Instead, we should realize God has gifted us in ways that line up with His purposes and be willing to let Him use those gifts to grow His kingdom.

BUILDING THE BRIDGE

Your bridge building efforts would result in failure if you were to leave out the Holy Spirit. That's why it is essential for you to rely on

His presence and power. You are not alone when it comes to bridge building; He resides in you to help you. You are equipped with not only His presence but with gifts that you can use as you engage in bridge building with others. When things get difficult—and they probably will—you should lean on Him. And when things are good, you should lean on Him. No matter what, recognize His presence in your life and His ability to transform you so that God can make you the best bridge builder you can possibly be.

QUESTIONS FOR REFLECTION AND DISCUSSION

1. How have you seen the gifts of the Holy Spirit manifested in your own life?

2. If someone asked you to explain the Holy Spirit, what would you say?

3. Can you describe a time when you were sure that you were being empowered by the Holy Spirit?

4. Read the lists of spiritual gifts in 1 Corinthians 12:8-10 and Romans 12:6-8. What spiritual gifts seem to be present in your life?

RECOMMENDED RESOURCES

A.W. Tozer, *How to Be Filled with the Holy Spirit* (Chicago, IL: Moody Publishers, 2016)

A.W. Tozer, *The Knowledge of the Holy: The Attributes of God: Their Meaning in the Christian Life* (San Francisco: HarperOne, 2009)

Charles F. Stanley, *Living in the Power of the Holy Spirit* (Nashville, TN: Thomas Nelson, 2005)

BUILDING THE BRIDGE WITH JEHOVAH'S WITNESSES[1]

S etting: your home on a Saturday morning in early fall. You hear the doorbell ring, and immediately you dread that your blinds are open because your visitors surely know you are home. You could ignore the ringing, or you could answer the door. You choose the latter, and you find yourself face to face with two Jehovah's Witnesses. Now what?

One of the basic principles of bridge building is preparation. Our hope should be that we have thoughtful engagement with people from all cultures and backgrounds and that people walk away from us knowing more about or feeling closer to Jesus. In order to engage thoughtfully with people from other worldviews, we should have some basic knowledge of their beliefs (see chapter 10). This doesn't mean we have to know everything about every religion, but we should at least be able to ask intelligent questions and share the core truths about Christianity.

WHY THEY'RE THERE

With regard to Jehovah's Witnesses (JWs) in particular, they have most assuredly prepared for their visit to your home. JWs spend time at their Kingdom Halls (what they call their church buildings) and study Scripture together, focusing on 1 Timothy 2:3-4 ("This is good, and pleases God our Savior, who wants all people to be saved and to come to a knowledge of the truth"), Acts 20:20 ("You know that I have not hesitated to preach anything that would be helpful to you but have taught you publicly and from house to house"), and 1 Peter 2:21 ("To this you were called, because Christ suffered for you, leaving you an example, that you should follow in his steps"). JWs use these verses as reminders that they are to boldly share their beliefs with others. And for those of us who are Christians, these verses should be part of the bedrock of why we evangelize.

In addition to using their Scriptures, JWs study a book called *Reasoning from the Scriptures*,[2] which prepares them for conversations about all sorts of topics, from abortion to celebrating birthdays to the Trinity. It also provides them answers they can give when challenged with statements like, "I'm not interested." Typically, their conversations begin with innocuous questions about the weather, and then the more they get to know you, the more serious their topics. Sort of like bridge building, but not quite because they aren't really trying to build a friendship with you at your front door. That might happen down the road as you begin to visit the Kingdom Hall and attend services with them. At your front door, however, they want to share the "good news" with you. (Careful: Their version of the good news is different than the biblical version of the good news.)

PHASE 1: THE START OF A RELATIONSHIP

Taking a page out of the apostle Paul's handbook on evangelism, JWs work to find common ground with you. You should respond in kind. *Don't be a jerk*—that's the last thing they need from Christians. Be a gracious host. You could even invite them in to have a real, bona fide conversation at your kitchen table (bonus points if you offer water and snacks). Be a missionary to the missionaries, so to speak.

My friend Cynthia Velasco Hampton, a former JW, suggests two phases for conversations with JWs: (1) the first meeting at your door, and (2) the established relationship. That first visit to your door or kitchen table is for the purpose of laying the groundwork for a relationship. They want to earn your trust, and you should want to earn theirs, through gracious conversation that shows a genuine interest in what they have to say. A couple of topics you'll want to avoid during that first meeting are discussions about cults or the Trinity.

Please don't tell anyone you just met that they are in a cult. That won't likely build a bridge, and you'll most likely get yourself blacklisted, which will likely cut off any opportunity you would have for further discussion. Talking about the Trinity is just as bad as telling them they are in a cult because they have been taught to "thought-stop" at the mention of the word *Trinity*. Thought-stopping is when a JW shuts down their brain and effectively leaves the conversation while still being physically present. They are no longer listening to you but are working toward finding a way to leave sooner rather than later. If you want to start laying some bricks to build a bridge, you could try these questions:

- **How did you become a JW?**

  This is a getting-to-know-you question. They might end up asking you why you became a Christian. Honestly, friends are getting to know friends here. Just have a normal, real conversation.

- **How do you know that the Watch Tower Society teaches truth?**

  You should have already answered this question for yourself regarding Christianity. Now you want to get the JWs thinking about why they believe what they believe.

- **Why is the Watch Tower Society called "the truth"?**

  Their founder, Charles Taze Russell, called the organization the truth, which is contrary to what Scripture says (Jesus is the truth, according to John 14:6).

- **When was the religion founded?**

  This can spark a conversation about the witnesses because they have likely been taught that they are the only true witnesses. But their organization was founded in 1872. Was God without a witness before 1872?

The first conversation you have with JWs will lay the foundation for what's to come. Either they will come back, or they won't. Either way, your conversation should encourage them to think deeply about what they believe and maybe reconsider what they've been taught about Christians (that we're unkind and unwilling to listen).

PHASE 2: FRIENDSHIP

As we learned in chapter 10, it is possible to be friends with people who have different worldviews. In fact, it can be fulfilling. Doing this with JWs might prove a bit difficult because they are not encouraged to be friends with people outside of their religion. That doesn't mean they won't be friendly, but it won't be easy. Be in constant prayer and remember to call on your *paraclete*, the Holy Spirit, to guide you at every turn.

Once you've had a few conversations with your new JW friends, your discussions will likely get deeper because that's the normal progression of friendship. They'll want to know more about you, and you'll want to know more about them. This isn't rocket science—you're just making friends and being a friend. If faith topics come up, great. If they don't, that's fine too. Continue to be a faithful Christ-follower in all that you think, do, and say. Your attitude and behavior will speak volumes.

If conversations about faith do arise, be aware that both Christians and JWs use some of the same terminology, but that doesn't mean we believe the same things. Always ask clarifying questions. Here are some you could ask:

- **Who is Jesus?**

  » JWs believe Jesus was Michael the Archangel.

  » JWs do not believe Jesus was divine, only that He had divine qualities.

  » JWs do not believe in the Trinity.

  » JWs believe Jesus is a minor god.

- **How can a person be saved?**

  JWs don't believe we're saved through what Jesus did by coming to earth, living, dying an awful death on the cross, paying the penalty for our sins, coming back to life after three days, and ascending to heaven to prepare a place for us. They also don't believe that we need merely to believe and accept forgiveness. Instead, they believe they earn their salvation through works.

- **What happens to people after death?**

  » JWs believe the "little flock" (made up of just 144,000 people) will get into heaven. All other JWs will be part of the "great crowd" and will remain in an earthly paradise for eternity.

  » All non-JWs will end up in Sheol (a common grave of

eternal unconsciousness). They do not believe in eternal punishment.

- **What is "New Light"?**

  JWs believe that the Watch Tower Society changes its opinion because of New Light—that is, new revelation from Jehovah. But Jesus is the light of the world, and truth is constant and unchanging.

No matter where your conversations go with Jehovah's Witnesses[3] or with people from any faith, including Christianity, enter with a heart of humility and a willingness to learn. Be unwaveringly kind. As Jesus told His disciples, "By this everyone will know that you are my disciples, if you love one another" (John 13:35). Take what you've learned from this book and apply it to every interaction you have.

Now go build bridges!

NOTES

FINDING THE RIGHT BALANCE WHEN YOU SHARE YOUR FAITH

1. I rewrote this introduction on May 19, 2023, the day Tim Keller passed away.

2. @Sipho_Mudau, Twitter, May 19, 2023, https://twitter.com/Sipho_Mudau/status/165963986 9415514113.

3. @dansadlier, Twitter, May 18, 2023, https://twitter.com/dansadlier/status/1659373131738349568.

4. @ChuckwFuller, Twitter, May 19, 2023, https://twitter.com/ChuckwFuller/status/165963952 9949593601.

5. @NeilThomas093, Twitter, May 19, 2023, https://twitter.com/NeilThomas093/status/16596400 46708719616.

6. @SteveElshaw, Twitter, May 19, 2023, https://twitter.com/SteveElshaw/status/165963754 6043998208.

7. Timothy Keller, *The Meaning of Marriage: Facing the Complexities of Commitment with the Wisdom of God* (New York: Penguin Books, 2011), 44.

8. @revmahoney, Twitter, May 19, 2023, https://twitter.com/revmahoney/status/1659635190 644310017.

9. This is partially adapted from my article "The Moment I Realized That Apologetics Was Important for Me as a Christian," *Mama Bear Apologetics*, https://mamabearapologetics.com/aha -moments/.

10. I'll define apologetics more substantially later, but for the sake of clarity, it means to give a defense.

11. A word of caution here: I know that not all familial relationships are warm, cozy, or healthy. You might need to put some barriers and boundaries in place, and that's okay. I'll address barriers and boundaries in chapter 13.

PART 1: THE ART OF BRIDGE BUILDING

1. This quote is widely attributed to H. Jackson Brown Jr.—the original source is unknown.

CHAPTER 1: BUT FIRST, LET'S PRAY

1. See Peter A. Boelens, Roy R. Reeves, et al., "A Randomized Trial of the Effect of Prayer on Depression and Anxiety," *International Journal of Psychiatry in Medicine* 39, no. 4 (2009): 377-392, doi:10.2190/PM.39.4.c.

2. Ryan H. Bremner, Sander L. Koole, et al, "'Pray for Those Who Mistreat You': Effects of Prayer on Anger and Aggression," *Personality & Social Psychology Bulletin* 37, no. 6 (2011): 830-837, doi:10.1177/0146167211402215.

3. Nathaniel M. Lambert, Frank D. Fincham, et al., "Motivating Change in Relationships: Can Prayer Increase Forgiveness?," *Psychological Science* 21, no. 1 (2010): 126-32, doi:10.1177/ 0956797609355634.

4. Peter Kreeft, *Prayer for Beginners* (San Francisco, CA: Ignatius Press, 2000), 15.

5. Angela Yang, "'Jeopardy' Fans Reel as 'Lord's Prayer' Question Goes Unanswered," *NBC News*, June 15, 2023, https://www.nbcnews.com/news/jeopardy-question-lord-prayer-hallowed-mayim-bialik-rcna89571.

6. Daniel Silliman, @danielsilliman, Twitter, June 16, 2023, https://twitter.com/danielsilliman/status/1669676948728197120.

7. See Paul Froese and Jeremy E. Uecker, "Prayer in America: A Detailed Analysis of the Various Dimensions of Prayer," *Journal for the Scientific Study of Religion* 61, issue 3-4 (September-December 2022): 663-689, https://doi.org/10.1111/jssr.12810; Heather Preston, "London: The UK's Most Prayerful Region According to Premier Survey," *Premier Christian News*, January 26, 2020, https://premierchristian.news/en/news/article/london-the-uk-s-most-prayerful-region-according-to-premier-survey.

8. John Yieh, "Lord's Prayer," *Oxford Bibliographies*, last updated April 26, 2018, https://www.oxfordbibliographies.com/view/document/obo-9780195393361/obo-9780195393361-0138.xml, accessed March 28, 2023.

9. Martin Luther, "A Simple Way to Pray," trans. Carl J. Schindler, in *Luther's Works*, vol. 43, ed. Gustav K. Wiencke (Philadelphia, PA: Fortress Press, 1968), 200.

10. James R. Nestingen, "The Lord's Prayer in *Luther's Catechism*," *Word and World* 22, no. 1 (Winter 2002), 41, https://wordandworld.luthersem.edu/content/pdfs/22-1_Lords_Prayer/22-1_Nestingen.pdf.

11. See R.C. Sproul, "What Does 'Coram Deo' Mean?," *Ligonier*, November 13, 2017, https://www.ligonier.org/learn/articles/what-does-coram-deo-mean.

12. Alistair Begg, *Pray Big: Learn to Pray Like an Apostle* (Charlotte, NC: The Good Book Company, 2019), 15.

13. "American Worldview Inventory 2020—At a Glance," Cultural Research Center at Arizona Christian University, August 4, 2020, https://www.arizonachristian.edu/wp-content/uploads/2020/08/AWVI-2020-Release-08-Perceptions-of-Sin-and-Salvation.pdf.

14. Eugene H. Peterson, *Working the Angles: The Shape of Pastoral Integrity* (Grand Rapids, MI: Eerdmans, 1987), 57.

15. Elmer L. Towns, *Praying the Psalms: To Touch God and Be Touched by Him* (Shippensburg, PA: Destiny Image Publishers, 2004), 11.

16. See "Lee and Leslie Strobel: Praying for Loved Ones," *lifetodaytv*, YouTube, January 31, 2018, https://www.youtube.com/watch?v=i2qtpvk86g0.

17. Andrew Murray, "The Prayer Life" in *Collected Works on Prayer* (New Kensington, PA: Whitaker House, 2013), 233.

CHAPTER 2: EVERYTHING YOU NEED TO KNOW
ABOUT BRIDGES (UNLESS YOU'RE AN ENGINEER)

1. "Overview of Bridges," 2021 Infrastructure Report Card, *American Society of Civil Engineers*, https://infrastructurereportcard.org/cat-item/bridges-infrastructure/.

2. "Evangelism Explosion Study of Americans' Openness to Talking About Faith," *Lifeway*

Research, 2022, https://research.lifeway.com/wp-content/uploads/2022/02/Evangelism-Explosion-Survey-of-Americans-Report.pdf.

3. For example, there's a bridge in Germany that was built in the 1970s yet neither side was completed so it remains a monument to unfinished business rather than a connection point. There's another bridge in New Jersey that is walled off on both sides, so it is an overpass and not a passageway. Finally, the McPhaul Suspension Bridge in Yuma, Arizona, is a bridge to nowhere because the highway moved, and there was no longer a need for it (except for the apparently large number of bees that inhabit it—there's a sign warning visitors about them).

4. David Blockley, *Bridges: The Science and Art of the World's Most Inspiring Structures* (New York: Oxford University Press, 2010), 11.

5. See Chris Woodward, "Bridges," *explain that stuff*, last updated February 13, 2022, https://www.explainthatstuff.com/bridges.html.

6. "Monthly Traffic Crossings," *Golden Gate Bridge Highway & Transportation District*, accessed May 26, 2023, https://www.goldengate.org/bridge/history-research/statistics-data/monthly-traffic-crossings/.

7. "Infrastructure Brooklyn Bridge," *New York City DOT*, accessed May 26, 2023, https://www.nyc.gov/html/dot/html/infrastructure/brooklyn-bridge.shtml.

8. "Sunshine Skyway Bridge, Florida, US," *Road Traffic Technology*, accessed May 26, 2023, https://www.roadtraffic-technology.com/projects/sunshine-skyway-bridge-florida/.

9. Linda Figg in Judith Dupré, *Bridges: A History of the World's Most Spectacular Spans* (New York: Black Dog & Leventhal Publishers, 2017), 1.

10. If you haven't seen the historical footage, the YouTube channel *Practical Engineering* has an excellent video about it. See "Why the Tacoma Narrows Bridge Collapsed," *Practical Engineering*, August 28, 2018, YouTube, 8:47, https://www.youtube.com/watch?v=mXTSnZgrfxM.

11. If you want to learn about other bridge collapses, there's a list you can access on Wikipedia that is quite helpful. See https://en.wikipedia.org/wiki/List_of_bridge_failures. See also Arturo E. Schultz, Alesso Pipinato, and Andrew J. Gastineau, "Bridge Collapse," in *Innovative Bridge Design Handbook: Construction, Rehabilitation and Maintenance*, ed. Allesio Pipinato (2021), 951-81, ProQuest Ebook Central.

12. "Bridges," 2021 Report Card for America's Infrastructure, *American Society of Civil Engineers*, https://infrastructurereportcard.org/wp-content/uploads/2020/12/Bridges-2021.pdf.

13. Blockley, *Bridges*, 115.

14. See "Bridges," 2021 Report Card for America's Infrastructure, *American Society of Civil Engineers*, https://infrastructurereportcard.org/cat-item/bridges-infrastructure/.

15. Manasee Wagh, "The I-95 Collapse Is a Tragic Reminder That U.S. Bridges Are Still Built Without Fire Safety in Mind," June 6, 2023, *Popular Mechanics*, https://www.popularmechanics.com/technology/infrastructure/a44201682/what-could-have-prevented-i-95-bridge-collapse/.

16. Figg, *Bridges*, 9.

CHAPTER 3: APOLOGETICS—A BRIDGE IN NEED OF REPAIR?

1. Matt Slick, "What Is the Role of Apologetics in Evangelism?" *Christian Apologetics and Research Ministry*, January 21, 2013, https://carm.org/evangelism/what-is-the-role-of-apologetics-in-evangelism/#.

2. I still have it, and years later when I looked at the bibliography, I noticed some familiar names in it, including a couple of my seminary professors.

3. The Appendix contains a helpful guide that may help you when Jehovah's Witnesses visit your home. It's an excerpt from an article I wrote for Mama Bear Apologetics in 2018.

4. Erik's blog is still publicly available, but he has asked that it be taken down from the site following a conversation he had with Jon. Out of respect to Erik and Jon, I will not link to the blog here.

5. I requested permission from both Erik and Jon to share this series of posts, which are still publicly available on X. They both graciously said yes, and each one had nothing but kind words to say of the other.

6. I asked for specific examples of the "nicest apologists" on X, and Real Atheology recommended the following: Joshua Rasmussen (@worldviewdesign), Dolores G. Morris (@doloresgmorris), and Kenny Pearce (@kennethlpearce), among others. One takeaway from the response is that atheists are paying attention to the good and the bad and are more than happy to highlight the good if asked.

7. Jerram Barr in Francis Schaeffer, *He Is There and He Is Not Silent*, 30th anniversary ed. (Wheaton, IL: Tyndale, 2001), xviii.

CHAPTER 4: BRIDGES + APOLOGETICS
= BRIDGE-BUILDING APOLOGETICS

1. Bruce D. Perry and Maia Szalavitz, *The Boy Who Was Raised by a Dog and Other Stories from a Child Psychiatrist's Notebook* (New York: Basic Books, 2006), 80.

2. Nalini Ambady and John J. Skowronski, ed., *First Impressions* (New York: Guilford Press, 2008), 2. "Social cognition refers to the processes through which people perceive, interpret, remember, and apply information about themselves and the social world. These processes are often relatively automatic in nature and therefore not fully within conscious awareness." Paula S. Nurius, "Cognition and Social Cognitive Theory," *Encyclopedia of Social Work* (June 2013), https://oxfordre.com/socialwork/view/10.1093/acrefore/9780199975839.001.0001/acrefore-9780199975839-e-65.

3. Ambady and Skowronski, *First Impressions*, 9.

4. Chris Voss with Tahl Raz, *Never Split the Difference: Negotiating as If Your Life Depended on It* (London: Random House, 2016), 32.

5. See J.Z. Siegel, C. Mathys et al., "Beliefs About Bad People Are Volatile," *Nature Human Behavior* 2 (2018): 750-756; and Scott Mautz, "A New Yale Study Says You Can Overcome a Bad First Impression by Doing This 1 Simple Thing," *Inc.*, October 29, 2018, https://www.inc.com/scott-mautz/want-to-overcome-that-bad-first-impression-you-left-a-new-yale-study-says-do-this-1-simple-thing.html.

6. See Marco Brambilla, Luciana Carraro et al., "Changing Impressions: Moral Character Dominates Impression Updating," *Journal of Experimental Social Psychology* 82 (May 2019): 64-73, doi:10.1016/j.jesp.2019.01.003.

7. Craig Blomberg, *Matthew*, The New American Commentary, ed. David S. Dockery (Nashville, TN: Broadman Press, 1992), 214.

8. Blomberg, *Matthew*, 215.

9. Blomberg, *Matthew*, 23.

10. Jeffery Fulks et al., "State of the Bible USA 2022," *American Bible Society*, https://1s712 .americanbible.org/state-of-the-bible/stateofthebible/State_of_the_bible-2022.pdf.

11. Barna Research, "Pastors Say They Often Preach on Church Unity—Christians Disagree," *Barna*, November 23, 2022, https://www.barna.com/research/pastors-christians-unity/.

12. David Platt, *Exalting Jesus in Matthew*, Christ-Centered Exposition Commentary, eds. David Platt, Daniel L. Akin, and Tony Merida (Nashville, TN: B&H Academic, 2013), 239-246.

13. Platt, *Exalting Jesus in Matthew*, 243.

14. Blomberg, *Matthew*, 278.

15. Blomberg, *Matthew*, 278.

16. Blomberg, *Matthew*, 100.

17. Jim Taylor, "3 Keys to Resolving Conflict," *Psychology Today*, August 29, 2019, https://www .psychologytoday.com/us/blog/the-power-prime/201908/3-keys-resolving-conflict.

CHAPTER 5: JESUS, THE ULTIMATE BRIDGE BUILDER

1. "Benefits of Youth Sports," PCSFN Science Board, *Health.gov*, September 17, 2020, https:// health.gov/sites/default/files/2020-09/YSS_Report_OnePager_2020-08-31_web.pdf.

2. For more information about the connection between faith and sports, I recommend the Faith and Sports Institute, https://truettseminary.baylor.edu/programs-centers/faith-sports-institute.

3. N.T. Wright, "The Mission and Message of Jesus," in *The Meaning of Jesus: Two Visions* (New York: HarperCollins, 1999), 37-38.

4. Wright, "The Mission and Message of Jesus," 38 (emphasis in original).

5. Due to copyright issues, I can't give you the words of the song here, but you can find it on the internet. It's worth the search if you've not heard it before!

6. Darrell L. Bock, *Luke*, The NIV Application Commentary (Grand Rapids, MI: Zondervan, 1996), 481.

7. Bock, *Luke*, 481.

8. This example serves another purpose. The one who returned to Jesus to give thanks was a Samaritan. I'll talk more about why this was such an extraordinary circumstance in chapter 10, "Interacting with People of Different Worldviews."

9. Jesus' interaction with babies in Matthew 19 should not have come as a surprise to the disciples because this wasn't the only time He interacted with children. In Matthew 18, He calls a child up and calls His followers to be "like little children" (verse 3).

10. William Steuart McBirnie, *The Search for the Twelve Apostles*, rev. ed. (Carol Stream, IL: Tyndale House, 1973), 24.

11. I reviewed this excellent book for *Christianity Today*. See Lindsey Medenwaldt, "Who Do You Say He Is?," *Christianity Today*, November 21, 2022, https://www.christianitytoday.com/ ct/2022/december/rebecca-mclaughlin-confronting-jesus-encounters-hero-gospel.html.

CHAPTER 6: PAUL, THE GOSPEL-CENTRIC BRIDGE BUILDER

1. Craig L. Blomberg, *Making Sense of the New Testament*, Three Crucial Questions series (Grand Rapids, MI: Baker Academic, 2004), 105-106.

2. I realize that some readers may not know what a Rolodex is. It's an old-school filing system for organizing business cards. It's like the small version of a Trapper Keeper.

3. The Greek word translated "set apart," *aphōrismenos*, means to mark off with boundaries. There was a clear demarcation between Paul's life before and after his encounter on the Damascus Road.

4. Robert H. Gundry, *A Survey of The New Testament* (Grand Rapids, MI: Zondervan, 1994), 81-82.

5. There are some different interpretations as to what Paul is referring to as his thorn here, including his opponents, his pain related to people rejecting the gospel, and a literal physical ailment. Whatever the thorn was, it caused him intense agony, not just slight discomfort.

6. One quick search on Quora reminded me of just how intolerant so-called tolerant people can be all the while claiming that Christians are the intolerant ones. See, for example, the answers to "What's more intolerant, not accepting someone's lifestyle or assuming everyone should agree to and support your lifestyle choices? Are they equally narrow-minded?," quora .com/Whats-more-intolerant-not-accepting-someones-lifestyle-or-assuming-everyone-should-agree-to-and-support-your-lifestyle-choices-Are-they-equally-narrow-minded, accessed April 24, 2023. It is clear from some of the answers that Christians have a lot of work to do as far as building bridges, at least in the minds of some non-Christians.

7. Warren W. Wiersbe, *On Being a Leader for God* (Grand Rapids, MI: Baker Books, 2011), 39.

8. Penn Jillette, "A Gift of a Bible," July 8, 2010, *beinzee*, YouTube, video, 5:11, https://www .youtube.com/watch?v=6md638smQd8.

9. Jillette, "A Gift of a Bible."

10. Thanks to Tammy Hulbert for the reminder to pray and make people my favorite.

CHAPTER 7: OTHER BRIDGE-BUILDING LESSONS FROM SCRIPTURE AND MODERNITY

1. Dietrich Bonhoeffer, *The Cost of Discipleship*, rev. and unabridged ed. (New York: Macmillan, 1979), 205-206.

2. Robert Penn Warren, *The Legacy of the Civil War* (Lincoln, NE: University of Nebraska Press, 1961), 100.

3. Scot McKnight, *Galatians*, The NIV Application Commentary (Grand Rapids, MI: Zondervan, 1995), 112.

4. "Two-Thirds of Christians Face Doubt," *Barna*, July 25, 2017, https://www.barna.com/research/two-thirds-christians-face-doubt/.

5. Brandon Washington, *A Burning House: Redeeming American Evangelicalism by Examining Its History, Mission, and Message* (Grand Rapids, MI: Zondervan, 2023), 202.

6. Washington, *A Burning House*, 211.

7. "Read Martin Luther King Jr.'s 'I Have a Dream' Speech in Its Entirety," *NPR*, updated January 16, 2023, https://www.npr.org/2010/01/18/122701268/i-have-a-dream-speech-in-its-entirety.

8. "Read Martin Luther King Jr.'s 'I Have a Dream' Speech in Its Entirety," *NPR*.

9. Nabeel Qureshi, "Vlog 43—Love and Peace are our Motivation," *Michelle Qureshi Wilson*, September 9, 2017, YouTube, 3:14, https://www.youtube.com/watch?v=zU9fu-lC3fY.

10. Qureshi, "Vlog 43—Love and Peace are our Motivation."

11. Nabeel Qureshi, "Nabeel Qureshi // Facing death threats after I left Islam for Christ," *Premier On Demand*, June 27, 2016, YouTube, 1:49, https://www.youtube.com/watch?v=81OLl2ithZ8.

12. Nabeel Qureshi, *No God But One: A Former Muslim Investigates the Evidence for Islam & Christianity* (Grand Rapids, MI: Zondervan, 2016), 294.

13. This became the title of her best-selling book, which was published in 1971.

14. "Corrie ten Boom," *Biography*, updated June 5, 2020, https://www.biography.com/activists/corrie-ten-boom.

15. Kathryn J. Atwood, *Women Heroes of World War II: 26 Stories of Espionage, Sabotage, Resistance, and Rescue* (Chicago, IL: Chicago Review Press, 2011), 122.

16. Atwood, *Women Heroes of World War II*, 119.

17. Corrie ten Boom, "Guideposts Classics: Corrie ten Boom on Forgiveness," *Guideposts*, https://guideposts.org/positive-living/guideposts-classics-corrie-ten-boom-forgiveness/.

PART 2: BECOMING A BRIDGE BUILDER

1. Greville MacDonald, *George MacDonald and His Wife* (New York: The Dial Press, 1924), 155.

CHAPTER 8: FIRM FOUNDATION 1—TRUTH

1. Lindsey Medenwaldt, "Ancient Aliens and the Bible: What the Popular Television Series Says about Extraterrestrials in Scripture," *Christian Research Journal*, last updated March 20, 2023, https://www.equip.org/articles/ancient-aliens-and-the-bible-what-the-popular-television-series-says-about-extraterrestrials-in-scripture/.

2. Lindsey Medenwaldt, "'Ancient Aliens,' Pyramids, and the Great Sphinx of Giza: Testing the Television Show's Claims with Truth," *Christian Research Journal*, last updated July 7, 2023, https://www.equip.org/articles/ancient-aliens-pyramids-and-the-great-sphinx-of-giza-testing-the-television-shows-claims-with-truth/.

3. Elon Musk, @elonmusk, Twitter, July 30, 2020, https://twitter.com/elonmusk/status/1289051795763769345. What's most troubling about the tweet for me was that it received 473,000 likes and more than 58,000 retweets. Compare this with his later tweet calling an article from the BBC that debunked claims extraterrestrials built the pyramids "sensible"—it received a mere 15,800 likes. Musk, @elonmusk, July 31, 2020, Twitter, https://twitter.com/elonmusk/status/1289408490205614080.

4. This is illogical and is contrary to what we find in Scripture. See Eric Geiger, "Can We Please Stop Saying 'My Truth'?," *The Gospel Coalition*, October 7, 2019, https://www.thegospelcoalition.org/article/stop-saying-my-truth/.

5. See Aaron Earls, "Almost All Churches and Most Churchgoers Are Now Gathering in Person," *Lifeway Research*, November 2, 2021, https://research.lifeway.com/2021/11/02/almost-all-churches-and-most-churchgoers-are-now-gathering-in-person/.

6. This section was inspired by Lindsey Medenwaldt, "Religious Pluralism," Profile, *Watchman Fellowship*, https://www.watchman.org/ProfileReligiousPluralism.pdf.

7. Lesslie Newbigin, *The Gospel in a Pluralist Society* (Grand Rapids, MI: Eerdmans, 1989), 14.

8. "Competing Worldviews Influence Today's Christians," *Barna*, May 9, 2017, https://www.barna.com/research/competing-worldviews-influence-todays-christians/.

9. "Competing Worldviews Influence Today's Christians," *Barna*.

10. This section is partially adapted from Lindsey Medenwaldt, "What Do New Agers Believe?" *Mama Bear Apologetics*, accessed July 23, 2023, https://mamabearapologetics.com/what-do-new-agers-believe/; and Lindsey Medenwaldt, "10 Questions You've Always Had About the New Age," *Mama Bear Apologetics*, accessed July 23, 2023, https://mamabearapologetics.com/new-age-q-and-a/.

11. For more on this trend see Lindsey Medenwaldt, "#Witchtok-Sorcery at Your Fingertips," *Christian Research Journal*, last updated June 21, 2023, https://www.equip.org/articles/witchtok-sorcery-at-your-fingertips/.

12. See Gabriella Raffetto, "Zealots, Zodiacs, and Zazen: Gen Z and Spirituality," *34th Street*, April 15, 2021, last accessed July 23, 2023, https://www.34st.com/article/2021/04/zealots-zodiacs-and-zazen-the-new-age-movement-and-what-spirituality-looks-like-today.

13. Elliot Miller, *A Crash Course in the New Age Movement* (Grand Rapids, MI: Baker, 1989), 186.

14. Aaron Earls, "Half of U.S. Protestant Pastors Hear Conspiracy Theories in Their Churches," *Lifeway Research*, January 26, 2021, https://research.lifeway.com/2021/01/26/half-of-u-s-protestant-pastors-hear-conspiracy-theories-in-their-churches/.

15. See Jan-Willem van Prooijen and Karen M. Douglas, "Belief in Conspiracy Theories: Basic Principles of an Emerging Research Domain," *European Journal of Social Psychology* 48, no. 7 (2018): 897-908, doi:10.1002/ejsp.2530.

16. See Benjamin J. Dow, Amber L. Johnson et al., "The COVID-19 Pandemic and the Search for Structure: Social Media and Conspiracy Theories," *Social and Personality Psychology Compass* 15 (9) (2021), doi:0.1111/spc3.12636.

17. The fake account @ericareport has since been suspended by X after a slew of other accounts called it out as being a bot (AI).

18. Matt Brown, *Truth Plus Love: The Jesus Way to Influence* (Grand Rapids, MI: Zondervan, 2019), 47.

19. Brown, *Truth Plus Love*, 203.

20. Cornelius Plantinga Jr., *Not the Way It's Supposed to Be: A Breviary of Sin* (Grand Rapids, MI: Eerdmans, 1995), 10.

21. Douglas Groothuis, *Christian Apologetics: A Comprehensive Case for Biblical Faith* (Downers Grove, IL: InterVarsity Press, 2011), 598.

CHAPTER 9: FIRM FOUNDATION 2—FRIENDSHIP

1. Rebecca McLaughlin, *No Greater Love: A Biblical Vision for Friendship* (Chicago, IL: Moody, 2023), 14.

2. Richard Wolf, "Opera, travel, food, law: The unlikely friendship of Ruth Bader Ginsburg and Antonin Scalia," *USA Today*, September 20, 2020, https://www.usatoday.com/story/news/politics/2020/09/20/supreme-friends-ruth-bader-ginsburg-and-antonin-scalia/5844533002/. See also James Rosen, *Scalia: Rise to Greatness, 1936–1986* (Washington, DC: Regnery, 2023), especially pages 298-304 and 399-402.

3. Christopher Scalia, "How Ginsburg and Scalia Maintained Their Friendship Amid Professional Differences," *PBS Newshour*, September 25, 2020, YouTube, 5:02, https://www.youtube.com/watch?v=uPgvuT-Ysks.

4. Wolf, "Opera, travel, food, law: The unlikely friendship of Ruth Bader Ginsburg and Antonin Scalia."

5. Wolf, "Opera, travel, food, law: The unlikely friendship of Ruth Bader Ginsburg and Antonin Scalia."

6. Rodney King made this statement in the wake of the 1992 Los Angeles riots. See https://www.youtube.com/watch?v=kKj4L6GwL5Y.

7. Christos Pezirkianidis, Evangelia Galanaki et al., "Adult Friendship and Wellbeing: A Systematic Review with Practical Implications," *Frontiers in Psychology* 14 (2023), https://doi.org/10.3389/fpsyg.2023.1059057.

8. Mayo Clinic Staff, "Friendships: Enrich Your Life and Improve Your Health," *Mayo Clinic*, January 12, 2022, https://www.mayoclinic.org/healthy-lifestyle/adult-health/in-depth/friendships/art-20044860. See also Karmel W. Choi, Murray B. Stein et al., "An Exposure-Wide and Mendelian Randomization Approach to Identifying Modifiable Factors for the Prevention of Depression," *American Journal of Psychiatry* 177, no. 10 (October 2020), doi:10.1176/appi.ajp.2020.19111158.

9. Pezirkianidis and Galanaki et al., "Adult Friendship and Wellbeing: A Systematic Review with Practical Implications."

10. Daniel A. Cox, "The State of American Friendship: Change, Challenges, and Loss," *Survey Center on American Life*, June 8, 2021, https://www.americansurveycenter.org/research/the-state-of-american-friendship-change-challenges-and-loss/.

11. See "COVID-19 Pandemic Led to Increase in Loneliness Around the World," *American Psychological Association*, May 9, 2022, https://www.apa.org/news/press/releases/2022/05/covid-19-increase-loneliness, and "The Pandemic Loosens Its Grip, but Loneliness Epidemic Keeps a Tight Hold," *OSF Healthcare*, February 17, 2023, https://newsroom.osfhealthcare.org/the-pandemic-loosens-its-grip-but-loneliness-epidemic-keeps-a-tight-hold/.

12. Myers-Briggs Type Indicator. In case you're wondering, I'm an INTJ. Essentially that means I enjoy solitude and order (though my husband will probably tell you I enjoy order in *theory*, not in *reality*). Being an introvert presents some potential struggles in the bridge-building department, but Jesus told us to make disciples. He didn't offer any caveats for personality types.

13. See Jennie Bedsworth, "Here Are 9 Ways to Make Friends as an Adult," *GoodRX Health*, May 20, 2022, https://www.goodrx.com/health-topic/mental-health/how-to-make-friends-as-an-adult.

14. See, for example, Lara Walsh, "These 2 Fans Met at a 2008 JoBros Concert, Now They'll Be BFFs 'Til the Year 3000," *Elite Daily*, October 27, 2021, https://www.elitedaily.com/lifestyle/best-friends-met-at-jonas-brothers-concert.

15. I happen to remember this specific night because it was the first time I saw my future husband, Jay, play hockey.

16. See, for example, Håvard Bergesen Dalen and Ørnulf Seippel, "Friends in Sports: Social Networks in Leisure, School and Social Media," *International Journal of Environmental Research and Public Health* 18 (June 2021): 6197, doi:10.3390/ijerph18126197; and Marie Høstrup Andersen, Laila Ottesen et al., "The Social and Psychological Health Outcomes of Team Sport Participation in Adults: An Integrative Review of Research," *Scandinavian Journal of Public Health* 47/8 (2019): 832-50, doi:10.1177/1403494818791405.

17. See Brandon Mastromartino and James J. Zhang, "Affective Outcomes of Membership in a Sport Fan Community," *Frontiers in Psychology* 11 (May 2020): 881, doi:10.3389/fpsyg.2020.00881; and Ellen Diamond, "The Psychology of Watching Sports: What Fans Get from Watching Football," *Psychreg*, last updated February 9, 2023, https://www.psychreg.org/psychology-watching-sports-what-fans-get-watching-football/.

18. Darius K.-S. Chan & Grand H.-L. Cheng, "A Comparison of Offline and Online Friendship Qualities at Different Stages of Relationship Development," *Journal of Social and Personal Relationships* 21, no. 3 (2004): 304-20, doi:10.1177/0265407504042834.

19. See Patti M. Valkenburg and Jochen Peter, "Preadolescents' and Adolescents' Online Communication and Their Closeness to Friends," *Developmental Psychology* 43, no. 2 (2007):267-277, doi:10.1037/0012-1649.43.2.267. This correlation seems to just get better with age.

20. See John F. Helliwell and Haifang Huang, "Comparing the Happiness Effects of Real and On-Line Friends," *PloS one* 8/9 (2013), doi:10.1371/journal.pone.0072754.

21. "American Time Use Survey," *U.S. Bureau of Labor Statistics*, last updated September 17, 2021, https://www.bls.gov/opub/hom/atus/pdf/atus.pdf. As I note in this chapter, however, sometimes entertainment can bring new friends together.

22. See "The Friendship Report 2020," Executive Summary, Alter Agents and Snapchat, https://images.ctfassets.net/inb32lme5009/5MJXbvGtFXFXbdofsiYbp/f24adc95cfad109994ebb8f9467bc842/Snap_Inc._The_Friendship_Report_2020_-Global-.pdf.

23. Hank Green, "How Do Adults Make Friends?," *vlogbrothers*, August 3, 2018, YouTube, 3:59, https://www.youtube.com/watch?v=fJIWMTWojy8.

24. Green, "How Do Adults Make Friends?"

25. Dale Carnegie & Associates, *How To Win Friends & Influence People in the Digital Age* (New York: Simon & Schuster, 2011), Part 3.

26. Chris Crandall, "Study Finds Our Desire for 'Like-Minded Others' Is Hard-Wired," *The University of Kansas*, February 23, 2016, http://news.ku.edu/2016/02/19/new-study-finds-our-desire-minded-others-hard-wired-controls-friend-and-partner.

27. Carnegie, *How to Win Friends & Influence People in the Digital Age*, 222.

28. Amy Hall, "Don't Sacrifice Truth. Instead, Make This Your Goal," *Stand to Reason*, May 8, 2023, YouTube, 0:59, https://www.youtube.com/watch?v=iYCE5lbHcjE.

29. See the children's book by Frieda Wishinsky & Natalie Nelson, *How Emily Saved the Bridge* (Toronto: Groundwood Books, 2019).

30. See, for example, Tresa Baldas, "Friends: Jehovah's Witnesses Shunning Drove Keego Harbor Mom to Murder-Suicide," *Detroit Free Press*, last updated February 20, 2018, https://www.freep.com/story/news/local/michigan/2018/02/19/keego-harbor-jehovahs-witness-mom-triple-murder-suicide/351559002/; Rosie Luther, "What Happens to Those Who Exit Jehovah's

Witnesses: An Investigation of the Impact of Shunning," *Pastoral Psychology* 72, no. 1 (2023): 105-120, doi:10.1007/s11089-022-01051-x.

31. A note of caution: *Welcome to Wrexham* contains a lot of foul language.

32. Another note of caution: as with *Welcome to Wrexham*, *Ted Lasso* has foul language. *Ted Lasso* also contains some explicit scenes, particularly after Season 1. I wish the producers of the show had stuck with their formula from Season 1 for all three seasons, but alas, they did not. As such, I can't stand behind the series as a whole, but I can still recognize the thread of goodness woven throughout because of the mostly positive example of Ted Lasso. Like my Mama Bear Apologetics friends say, let's chew and spit—that is, let's keep the good and get rid of the bad.

33. Mark Travers, "2 Ways to Stay Friends with People Who Have Strong Opinions," *Psychology Today*, February 7, 2023, https://www.psychologytoday.com/us/blog/social-instincts/202302/2 -ways-to-stay-friends-with-people-who-have-strong-opinions.

34. Dietrich Bonhoeffer in *Called to Community: The Life Jesus Wants for His People*, ed. Charles E. Moore (Walden, NY: Plough Publishing, 2016), 134.

35. *Selected Addresses and Public Papers of Woodrow Wilson*, ed. Albert Bushnell Hart (New York: The Modern Library, 1918), 258.

CHAPTER 10: INTERACTING WITH PEOPLE OF DIFFERENT WORLDVIEWS

1. @Goodbye_Jesus, Twitter, May 16, 2023, https://twitter.com/Goodbye_Jesus/status/16584560 91670315008.

2. @Kapteinn_Nemo, Twitter, May 17, 2023, https://twitter.com/Kapteinn_Nemo/status/16590183 91376519172.

3. "The State of Theology," *Lifeway Research, 2022*, https://thestateoftheology.com/.

4. I recommend browsing the entire report from Lifeway. There is even an option to take the sur- vey yourself to see where you land. It might prove to be an enlightening exercise.

5. This is adapted from my article "A Crash Course in Christian Doctrine," *Mama Bear Apologet- ics*, accessed July 23, 2023, https://mamabearapologetics.com/crash-course-christian-doctrine/.

6. For a quick video about the historical reliability of the Old Testament, I suggest "Why Is the Bible Reliable? | Tim Keller at Columbia University," *The Veritas Forum*, November 29, 2011, YouTube, video, 5:37, https://youtu.be/UZAPFKXMy_Y. For a short video about the reliabil- ity of the New Testament, I recommend "For the City: Craig L. Blomberg on 'The Reliability of the New Testament,'" *Denver Seminary*, August 3, 2017, YouTube, video, 1:14:00, https:// youtu.be/rhPlg_p9TDY.

7. Dalai Lama, quoted in Winfried Corduan, *Neighboring Faiths: A Christian Introduction to World Religions*, 2d ed. (Downers Grove, IL: InterVarsity, 2012), 57.

8. Corduan, *Neighboring Faiths*, 57.

9. Amy Hall, "Approaching Spiritual Conversations—Classic—Amy Hall, Greg Koukl, and Mikel Del Rosario," *thetablepodcast*, YouTube, video, 56:50, https://youtu.be/clcX6ZecPuM.

10. Douglas Groothuis, *Christian Apologetics: A Comprehensive Case for Biblical Faith* (Downers Grove, IL: IVP Academic, 2011), 44.

11. See Adrian F. Ward, "The Neuroscience of Everybody's Favorite Topic," *The Scientific American*,

July 16, 2013, https://www.scientificamerican.com/article/the-neuroscience-of-everybody -favorite-topic-themselves/.

12. Julian Treasure, "5 Ways to Listen Better," *TEDGlobal*, July 2011, video, 7:34, https://www .ted.com/talks/julian_treasure_5_ways_to_listen_better.

13. Treasure, "5 Ways to Listen Better."

14. Corduan, *Neighboring Faiths*, 309.

15. See Gregory Koukl, *Tactics: A Game Plan for Discussing Your Christian Convictions*, 10th ed. (Grand Rapids, MI: Zondervan, 2019).

16. See Corduan, *Neighboring Faiths*, 352-356.

17. "Do Christians and LDS Believe The Same Thing?," *Finding Something Real Podcast*, replay posted February 15, 2023, https://podbay.fm/p/finding-something-real/e/1676454300.

CHAPTER 11: NAVIGATING CULTURAL DIVIDES

1. Rebecca McLaughlin, *Confronting Christianity: 12 Hard Questions for the World's Largest Religion* (Wheaton, IL: Crossway, 2019), 35.

2. This is the same mountain that Abraham and Isaac visited in Genesis 22. Samaritans regard the temple here as the true temple of Yahweh.

3. "Barbara Henry: The Teacher Who Helped Ruby Bridges Integrate a New Orleans School," *Chalkboard Champions*, August 18, 2020, https://chalkboardchampions.org/barbara-henry-the-teacher -who-helped-ruby-bridges-integrate-a-new-orleans-school/.

4. "Ruby Bridges," *Hilbert College*, accessed July 24, 2023, https://www.hilbert.edu/social-justice -activists/ruby-bridges.

5. Barbara Henry, "Civil Rights Pioneer on First-Grade Teacher: 'She Showed Me Her Heart' | Where Are They Now | OWN," *OWN*, December 31, 2014, YouTube, video, 2:08, https:// youtu.be/qwb5xsROlyc.

6. "Henry: The Teacher Who Helped Ruby Bridges Integrate a New Orleans School."

7. For more information about Americans and cancel culture, see Emily A. Vogels, Monica Anderson et al., "Americans and 'Cancel Culture': Where Some See Calls for Accountability, Others See Censorship, Punishment," *Pew Research Center*, May 19, 2021, https://www.pewresearch .org/internet/2021/05/19/americans-and-cancel-culture-where-some-see-calls-for-accountability -others-see-censorship-punishment/.

8. Pope Francis, "Address of His Holiness Pope Francis to the Members of the Diplomatic Corps Accredited to the Holy See," January 10, 2022, https://www.vatican.va/content/francesco/en/ speeches/2022/january/documents/20220110-corpo-diplomatico.html.

9. Max Zahn and Kiara Alfonseca, "Boycotts rarely work, experts say amid Bud Light anti-trans backlash," *ABC News*, April 14, 2023, https://abcnews.go.com/Business/boycotts-rarely-work -experts-amid-bud-light-anti/story?id=98538734.

10. Adam Liptak, "John Roberts Criticized Supreme Court Confirmation Process, Before There Was a Vacancy," *The New York Times*, March 21, 2016, https://www.nytimes.com/2016/03/22/ us/politics/john-roberts-criticized-supreme-court-confirmation-process-before-there-was-a- vacancy.html.

11. "Roll Call Vote 109th Congress—1st Session," https://www.senate.gov/legislative/LIS/roll_call_votes/vote1091/vote_109_1_00245.htm.

12. Taylor Orth, "Two in Five Americans Say a Civil War Is at Least Somewhat Likely in the Next Decade," *YouGov*, August 26, 2022, https://today.yougov.com/topics/politics/articles-reports/2022/08/26/two-in-five-americans-civil-war-somewhat-likely.

13. Orth, "Two in Five Americans."

14. Steven Olikara, "Our Post-Pandemic Democracy Needs Radical Bridge-Builders," *Millennial Action Project*, September 1, 2021, https://www.millennialaction.org/press-archives/our-post-pandemic-democracy-needs-radical-bridge-builders.

15. Patrick Schreiner, *Political Gospel: Public Witness in a Politically Crazy World* (Nashville, TN: B&H Publishing, 2022), 191.

16. Schreiner, *Political Gospel*, 193.

17. See Mark Home, "Christians, Anger Will Not Accomplish Our Political Goals," *Christian Post*, October 13, 2021, https://www.christianpost.com/news/christians-anger-will-not-accomplish-our-political-goals.html.

18. "Bridging Differences," *Greater Good Science Center*, last accessed July 24, 2023, https://ggsc.berkeley.edu/what_we_do/major_initiatives/bridging_differences.

19. Scott Shigeoka and Jason Marsh, "Eight Keys to Bridging Our Differences," *Greater Good Magazine*, July 22, 2020, https://greatergood.berkeley.edu/article/item/eight_keys_to_bridging_our_differences.

20. McLaughlin, *Confronting Christianity*, 45. See especially chapter 2, "Doesn't Christianity Crush Diversity?"

21. See Charlotte Huff, "Media Overload Is Hurting Our Mental Health. Here Are Ways to Manage Headline Stress," *Monitor on Psychology* 53, no. 8 (November 2022), https://www.apa.org/monitor/2022/11/strain-media-overload.

22. See Ron Carucci, "How to Build Bridges Between the Most Bitterly Divided People," *Forbes*, September 23, 2019, https://www.forbes.com/sites/roncarucci/2019/09/23/how-to-build-bridges-between-the-most-bitterly-divided-people/?sh=1578d9935ecd.

CHAPTER 12: RESPONDING TO THOSE WHO MAKE FUN OF CHRISTIANITY AND THE BIBLE

1. Martin Luther King Jr., "Loving Your Enemies," Sermon Delivered at Dexter Avenue Baptist Church, November 17, 1957, https://kinginstitute.stanford.edu/king-papers/documents/loving-your-enemies-sermon-delivered-dexter-avenue-baptist-church.

2. Susan Krauss Whitbourne, "How to Handle Someone Who Puts You Down," *Psychology Today*, April 3, 2021, https://www.psychologytoday.com/us/blog/fulfillment-any-age/202104/how-handle-someone-who-puts-you-down.

3. "David Cross—The Bible," *punchline magazine*, April 8, 2010, YouTube, 1:13, https://www.youtube.com/watch?v=CWOqHHE4upY.

4. For a deeper discussion about this, see Craig Blomberg, *Can We Still Believe the Bible? An Evangelical Engagement with Contemporary Questions* (Ada, MI: Brazos Press, 2014).

5. See Scott Rae and Thomas Sieberhage, "Portrayals of Committed Christians in Hollywood

Media," *Thinking Biblically* podcast, January 19, 2023, https://www.biola.edu/blogs/think
-biblically/2023/portrayals-of-committed-christians-in-hollywood-media. They also mention
that atheists are sometimes unfairly shown as harsh.

6. Reba Riley, "Losing My Religion: America's 'Post-Traumatic Church Syndrome,'" *Time*, May 19,
   2015, https://time.com/3859374/losing-my-religion-americas-post-traumatic-church-syndrome/.

7. Riley, "Losing My Religion: America's 'Post-Traumatic Church Syndrome.'"

8. Aaron Earls, "Christians Say They're More Likely to Forgive Than Be Forgiven," *Lifeway
   Research*, May 3, 2019, https://research.lifeway.com/2019/05/03/christians-say-theyre-more
   -likely-to-forgive-than-be-forgiven/.

9. Earls, "Christians Say They're More Likely to Forgive Than Be Forgiven."

10. "In Theory: Should religion be off limits to comedy?" *Glendale News-Press*, May 5, 2012, https://
    www.latimes.com/socal/glendale-news-press/opinion/tn-gnp-xpm-2012-05-05-tn-pas-0506
    -in-theory-should-religion-be-off-limits-to-comedy-story.html.

11. *The Babylon Bee* seems to provide a counterpoint to the comedy we find in media, at least
    according to editor-in-chief Kyle Mann. He unapologetically says, "We're going to continue
    to make fun of people, no matter if it's seen as punching up or punching down...Let's mock
    people who hold cultural power and let's communicate truth to a culture that many times
    does not believe in an objective, universal truth any longer." Emma Green, "The Christians
    Who Mock Wokeness for a Living," *The Atlantic*, October 14, 2021, https://www.theatlantic
    .com/politics/archive/2021/10/babylon-bee-news-kyle-mann-wokeism/620376/.

12. G.K. Chesterton, *All Things Considered* (New York: John Lane Company, 1920), 203.

13. See Peter J. Schuurman, "Faithful Laughter: C.S. Lewis, G.K. Chesterton, and Peter L. Berger on
    Faith and Comedy," *Sensus Divinitatis*, April 22, 2020, https://peterschuurman.ca/2020/04/22/
    faithful-laughter-c-s-lewis-g-k-chesterton-and-peter-l-berger-on-faith-and-comedy/; and Scot
    McKnight, "Humor as Theology," *Jesus Creed* blog, *Christianity Today*, December 31, 2019,
    https://www.christianitytoday.com/scot-mcknight/2019/december/humor-as-theology.html.

14. See "Quality Quarantine Day 20—#FunandFellowshipFriday Puppets," *Mama Bear Apologetics*,
    April 16, 2020, YouTube, video, 8:42, https://youtu.be/aE3VMgEl_aA. I assure you that hilarity
    ensues, but probably only because we were all stuck at home due to the COVID-19 pandemic.

CHAPTER 13: WHEN BARRIERS ARE NECESSARY—
GUARDRAILS AND BUMPERS

1. Ajith Fernando, *Acts*, The NIV Application Commentary, ed. Terry Muck (Grand Rapids, MI:
   Zondervan, 1998), 437.

2. Jackie Hill Perry, "The Importance of Boundaries," *Let's Talk*, The Gospel Coalition Podcast
   Network, February 2, 2022, https://www.thegospelcoalition.org/podcasts/lets-talk-podcast/
   boundaries/.

3. Henry Cloud and John Townsend, *Boundaries: When to Say Yes, How to Say No to Take Control of Your Life*, updated and expanded ed. (Grand Rapids, MI: Zondervan, 2017), 148.

4. For more about the value of friendships in church, see Anthony Salangsang, "The Importance of Friendship," *TableTalk*, June 2021, https://tabletalkmagazine.com/article/2021/06/
   the-importance-of-friendship/.

5. Ying Chen, Howard K. Koh et al., "Religious Service Attendance and Deaths Related to Drugs, Alcohol, and Suicide Among US Health Care Professionals," *JAMA Psychiatry* 77, no. 7:737-744, doi:10.1001/jamapsychiatry.2020.0175.

6. For more about the mentoring relationship between Paul and Barnabas, see Orlando Rivera, "Mentoring Stages in the Relationship between Barnabas and Paul," *Journal of Biblical Perspectives in Leadership* (2007), https://www.regent.edu/journal/journal-of-biblical-perspectives-in-leadership/mentoring-stages-in-the-relationship-between-barnabas-and-paul/.

7. Peter Englert, "A Prayer for the Bridgebuilders," September 13, 2020, https://peterenglert.com/a-prayer-for-the-bridgebuilders/.

CHAPTER 14: CONFIDENTLY SHARING YOUR FAITH

1. Scott Rae, *Moral Choices: An Introduction to Ethics* (Grand Rapids, MI: Zondervan, 2009), 42.

2. Rae, *Moral Choices*, 42.

3. Craig Blomberg, *1 Corinthians*, The NIV Application Commentary, ed. Terry Muck (Grand Rapids, MI: Zondervan, 1994), 264.

4. Andrea Zaccaro, Andrea Piarulli et al., "How Breath-Control Can Change Your Life: A Systematic Review on Psycho-Physiological Correlates of Slow Breathing," *Frontiers in Human Neuroscience* 12, no. 353 (September 2018), doi:10.3389/fnhum.2018.00353.

5. Allison Shapira, "Breathing Is the Key to Persuasive Public Speaking," *Harvard Business Review*, June 30, 2015, https://hbr.org/2015/06/breathing-is-the-key-to-persuasive-public-speaking.

6. Shapira, "Breathing Is the Key to Persuasive Public Speaking."

7. Gail MacDonald, *High Call, High Privilege: A Pastor's Wife Speaks to Every Woman in a Place of Responsibility* (Peabody, MA: Hendrickson Publishers, 1998), 36.

8. Rosaria Butterfield, *The Gospel Comes with a House Key: Practicing Radically Ordinary Hospitality in Our Post-Christian World* (Wheaton, IL: Crossway, 2018), 77.

9. Francis A. Schaeffer, *The Mark of the Christian*, 2d ed. (Downers Grove, IL: IVP Classics, 2006), 47-48.

10. See "Rosaria Butterfield and Ken Smith: An Unlikely Friendship and a Beautiful Conversion," *C.S. Lewis Institute*, April 5, 2021, YouTube, video, 1:45:14, https://www.youtube.com/watch?v=ipmlG_L9dvo.

11. Thanks, Katherine Allen, for this brilliant idea.

12. See chapters 8–11 in Andy Bannister, *How to Talk About Jesus Without Looking Like an Idiot: A Panic-Free Guide to Having Natural Conversations About Your Faith* (Carol Stream, IL: Tyndale, 2023).

13. "Research: Unchurched Will Talk About Faith, Not Interested in Going to Church," *Lifeway Research*, June 28, 2016, https://research.lifeway.com/2016/06/28/unchurched-will-talk-about-faith-not-interested-in-going-to-church/.

14. "Multigenerational Survey on Evangelism," *Jesus Film Project*, February 4, 2020, https://www.jesusfilm.org/blog/jfp-multigenerational-survey-evangelism/.

CHAPTER 15: LEAVE ROOM FOR THE HOLY SPIRIT

1. Michael F. Bird, *Evangelical Theology: A Biblical and Systematic Introduction* (Grand Rapids, MI: Zondervan, 2013), 611. This is a textbook, but if you're looking for an accessible book about theology, this is a great place to begin your studies. Plus, he's funny.

2. "Americans Continue to Redefine—and Reject—God," AWVI 2020 Results—Release #3: Perceptions of God, April 21, 2020, Cultural Research Center, Arizona Christian University, https://www.arizonachristian.edu/wp-content/uploads/2020/04/CRC-AWVI-2020 -Release-03_Perceptions-of-God.pdf.

3. Bird, *Evangelical Theology*, 613.

4. Ajith Fernando, *Acts*, The NIV Application Commentary (Grand Rapids, MI: Zondervan, 1998), 56.

APPENDIX: BUILDING THE BRIDGE WITH JEHOVAH'S WITNESSES

1. This is adapted and reproduced from my article "How to Talk to the Jehovah's Witness at Your Door," *Mama Bear Apologetics*, last accessed July 6, 2023, https://mamabearapologetics.com/ how-to-talk-to-the-jehovahs-witness-at-your-door/. Similar strategies described in this appendix can be applied to interactions with people from other worldviews.

2. This book is available for free online at the Jehovah's Witnesses website: https://www.jw.org/en/ library/books/Reasoning-From-the-Scriptures/. For a Christian response to this book, I recommend Ron Rhodes, *Reasoning from the Scriptures with the Jehovah's Witnesses*, rev. ed. (Eugene, OR: Harvest House, 2009).

3. For more information about the Jehovah's Witnesses, see Lindsey Medenwaldt, "Jehovah's Witnesses," in *The Popular Handbook of World Religions* (Eugene, OR: Harvest House, 2021).

To learn more about Harvest House books and
to read sample chapters, visit our website:

www.HarvestHousePublishers.com

HARVEST HOUSE PUBLISHERS
EUGENE, OREGON